CAMBRIDGE STREE]
Their Origins and Ass

This book draws on the great wealth of associations of street-names in Cambridge. It is not a dictionary but provides a series of entries on such topics as the Reformation, George IV and his wife, twentieth-century scientists, businessmen, Elizabethan times, medieval Cambridge, mayors, millers and builders. It includes hermits and coal merchants, field-marshals and laundresses, martyrs and bombers, unscrupulous politicians and the founder of a Christian community, Cromwell and Newton, an Anglo-Saxon queen, Stalin's daughter and the discoverer of Uranus – all people who lived in or often visited Cambridge.

The ancient Stourbridge Fair is included, along with castles and boat-races, sewage pumps and the original Hobson of 'Hobson's Choice'. Who was St Tibb? Where did Dick Turpin hide? Where was the medieval takeaway? Unlike earlier works, this is a history of everybody for everybody, not least for teachers, for whom the many references to other works will be helpful. The book also sheds light on such questions as which names are preferred, and how such choices may benefit the sociological study of Cambridge. The entries are spiced with anecdotes and epigrams, and a number of drawings by the architect and planner, Virén Sahai OBE, are included.

RONALD GRAY is a Fellow of Emmanuel College, Cambridge, having formerly been Vice-Master of the college and University Lecturer in German.

DEREK STUBBINGS writes and lectures on local history in Cambridge.

King's Parade

CAMBRIDGE STREET-NAMES

Their Origins and Associations

RONALD GRAY

AND

DEREK STUBBINGS

WITH ILLUSTRATIONS BY VIRÉN SAHAI

CAMBRIDGE
UNIVERSITY PRESS

PUBLISHED BY THE PRESS SYNDICATE OF THE UNIVERSITY OF CAMBRIDGE
The Pitt Building, Trumpington Street, Cambridge, United Kingdom

CAMBRIDGE UNIVERSITY PRESS
The Edinburgh Building, Cambridge CB2 2RU, UK   http://www.cup.cam.ac.uk
40 West 20th Street, New York, NY 10011-4211, USA   http://www.cup.org
10 Stamford Road, Oakleigh, Melbourne 3166, Australia
Ruiz de Alarcón 13, 28014 Madrid, Spain

First published 2000

Printed in the United Kingdom at the University Press, Cambridge

Typeface Monotype Fournier 12/15 pt   *System* QuarkXPress™   [SE]

A catalogue record for this book is available from the British Library

Library of Congress Cataloguing in Publication data
p. cm.

ISBN 0 521 78956 7 paperback

Contents

Contents

Acknowledgements

We are grateful to the staff of the Cambridgeshire Collection and the County Record Office, and above all to Mike Petty and Chris Jakes for unfailing help and courtesy; also to the staff of London Metropolitan Archives, Dr John Pickles, Dr F. H. Stubbings and the archivists of Trinity College, St John's College, Queens' College, St Catharine's College and Jesus College. Special thanks to Linda Allen for endless patience and thoughtful typing.

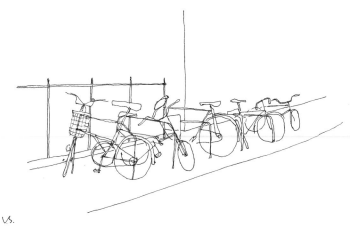

VS.

What do street-names mean?

Names are a sensitive matter: a 'wrong' name can affect the price of houses, as the residents of Barton Road realised on hearing the news of a fresh development, when they objected to the name Wortley, that of a seventeenth-century Fellow of Caius, as 'ugly and cumbersome to use'. St Neots residents objected recently to the names of councillors being given to streets, preferring those of local footballers. The vicar of a church in SUEZ* Road protested that 'Suez' was a dirty word politically (referring to the abortive Suez Canal attack of 1956): on the phone, people had thought he said 'sewers'. That name remains, but a proposal to call KIMBERLEY Road, with its South African name, after Nelson Mandela, was also vigorously opposed by residents, for whom, at that time, the great man was a Communist terrorist. His name survives in Mandela House in Regent Street, containing offices of the City Council.

Personal names were given frequently in the nineteenth century. Before that, streets were usually named according to goods sold in them – the medieval centre of Cambridge has no personal names except those of saints. Only later were any other individuals singled out to be honoured, although in paintings they appear as early as the thirteenth century.

Ribald and obscene names still found on nineteenth-century maps have almost all vanished, no doubt from concern with property prices. Who in fact ever did call TRINITY Lane

---

* Capitals are used for something of special interest about a street. Where some (varying) degree of doubt is present the name is enclosed in square brackets.

Pisspot Lane, however appropriate it may have been in less hygienic times? And how about Bandy Leg Walk, now demurely LADY MARGARET Road – was some resident being mocked? In BOTOLPH Lane, where there was a workhouse, mockery was certainly implied by the nickname Penny Farthing Lane.

A red light district existed in earlier times around NAPIER Street, to which MAIDS' CAUSEWAY led; it was renamed by some wag Coarse Maids Way. (The same wag, perhaps, turned SEDLEY TAYLOR Road into Tiddly Sailor Road.) Similarly, STOURBRIDGE has given rise to spurious etymology, re-spelling it as Sturbitch. Cambridge does not have, as some towns do, a Grape Road, whose vowel has been changed in the course of time, but the old name Hore Hill, also called Hare Hill, once graced an area round POUND Hill where prostitutes were still being arrested in the 1970s. (Oxford's Horspath, the first sylla-ble appearing also in the nearby Horsepath, seems to have had the same original meaning.) But Cambridge does have a Cut Throat Lane, not shown on maps, but well known in the Newmarket Road, and even used on the vans of a company selling pine furniture there, referring of course to its prices.

More respectably, but still in the interests of property, BERMUDA Road reassumed its delectable name when it changed from the awful industrial connotations of Foundry Road. Then there are OXFORD, RICHMOND, CAN-TERBURY, WINDSOR, all close together, streets which would never have been popular if Bradford, Swansea or Middlesbrough had been proposed – though HALIFAX slipped somehow into the same group of names that tourists fancy. Quite near to this are ARUNDEL, CLIVEDEN, WARWICK and several others with unquestionable status as castles and homes of the nobility, perhaps named by the same person. CROMWELL and FAIRFAX, however, on the other, eastern side of Cambridge, could have been deliberately sited for their radical associations. This was a 'Labour' area.

BELGRAVE is a decidedly 'posh' name, and there is something in the battlemented bay windows of Victorian terrace houses that still shows, in names like 'Chatsworth', 'Carltonia', 'Charterhouse', an apparent wish to be associated with the high and mighty. (Less concerned with such pretensions are the boarding house name 'Lingalonga', and the combinations of forenames: 'Louistan', 'Rondale', 'Rondoral'.) Other names favoured by somebody in charge suggest rural idylls, often in the Lake District, or in '-ferns' and '-dales', Scottish places (and a few Irish, but no Welsh) and in 'glens' and 'meads'. The prefix 'Lyn-' is curiously popular in house names. Religious personages are liked for reasons not hard to guess: 'abbot', 'bishop', 'friar', 'monk', 'nun' all occur, and there is romance in the many '-crofts' and '-holmes', '-hursts' and '-denes'. Yet who would choose to live in BUFFALO Way or yet MANDRILL Close, if offered an alternative? There is a regular zoo in the Cherry Hinton area, with names chosen by South Cambridgeshire District Council, against objections by the City Council, which preferred, and elsewhere got, local flower names, CLOVER, COLTSFOOT and so on. Almost all native trees occur.

Cambridge does not go in for foreign capitals, and hardly for foreign places at all. PORTUGAL, which once supplied port via nearby QUAYSIDE to college High Tables, and no doubt businessmen's tables too, is a rare exception. Apart from a few Empire names such as MADRAS, KIMBERLEY, PRETORIA and possibly BANFF and CALLANDER (but these two names are found in Scotland as well as in Canada), there are only

MANHATTAN and LEXINGTON, oddly enough, seeing that the latter is the place that saw the first defeat of the British in the American War of Independence, in 1775 – and of course TRAFALGAR, but not Waterloo; both NELSON and WELLINGTON were afforded pokey places compared with the grand thoroughfares in Paris named after Napoleon's marshals. (No one has thought Agincourt or Crécy suitable.) Churchill does not have a street named after him at all; even London has nothing comparable to the Avenue Charles de Gaulle. BLENHEIM, where Churchill lived, had to suffice, though a college is named after him.

Women's names rarely occur. Despite the growing confession that women have been unfairly treated by society, only eight were named in this century and recently there has even been a 'PRINCE WILLIAM' but no 'Princess Anne' or 'Princess of Wales'.

'Street' names are often road names. The change from one to the other is yet another sign of social preferences. As an official explained in the *Daily Telegraph* in 1971 (quoted by L. Dunkley in *The Guinness Book of Names*, p. 156): 'Streets have gone out of fashion and no one wants to live in one. When people think of a street they imagine something like the Coronation Street image of old terraced back-to-backs. You can call them roads, avenues, lanes, groves, drives, closes, places – anything but streets.' Cambridge follows the same trend; it has also 'causeway', 'broadway', 'corner', 'crescent', 'end', 'pightle', 'hill' (of all things), 'glebe', 'drift' and many more. But if you look at the centre, and at the nineteenth-century developments in the 'Kite' area, along Mill Road, the northern end of Hills Road, the Newnham and Romsey Town areas, you will seldom find any other designation but 'street', and in the newer areas hardly find it at all. 'Terrace', first noted by Charles Kingsley in 1851, according to the *Oxford English Dictionary*, as a name for suburban rows of houses, perhaps reflecting the glory of London's Carlton House Terrace, was an alternative to 'street' even at that time. But today the objection of house-buyers to 'street', and to 'terrace' as well, has vanished. The people who lived in such places were largely working class, railwaymen and college servants, and their successors have moved out to the suburbs, to Arbury, King's Hedges, Cherry Hinton, Histon, while the professional classes who want to be near the station or the city restaurants send sky-high the prices of what were sometimes slums.

Trinity Street

How can you tell?

Cambridge streets reflect the dominance of the University, though not so much as taxidrivers sometimes suppose. There are clusters of names especially in the area of TRUMPINGTON Road, COLERIDGE Road, GRANGE Road, MILL Road, QUEEN EDITH'S Way, BARTON Road, NEWNHAM and off HUNTINGDON Road, where each college holds or held land, often acquired in the nineteenth-century Inclosures.

The streets concerned here are:

Christ's: DARWIN, FRANCIS DARWIN, MILTON.

Churchill: COCKCROFT.

Clare: FERRARS, LATIMER.

Corpus Christi: MAWSON, TENISON, PEROWNE, EMERY, MACKENZIE, [WILKIN], PARKER, SPENS, GOUGH, STUKELY, MARLOWE.

Downing: LENSFIELD.

Emmanuel: ALEX WOOD, HOPKINS, PEMBERTON, FINCH, HOLLAND.

Gonville and Caius: GUEST, COLLIER, WILLIS, GONVILLE, MORTIMER, DROSIER, GRESHAM, HARVEY, GLISSON, BATEMAN, WOLLASTON, PERSE, SCROOPE.

Jesus: GREVILLE, CORRIE, RUSTAT, FLAMSTEED, FANSHAWE, BANCROFT, DAVY, RADEGUND, STERNE, CRANMER, FAIRBAIRN, [TILLYARD].

King's: KING'S (not King Street), KING'S PARADE, ANSTEY, MILLINGTON, CHEDWORTH, MERTON,

ELTISLEY, WALPOLE, [WEST], KEYNES, DURN-FORD.

Magdalene: [BUCKINGHAM], PEPYS.

Newnham: RACKHAM.

Pembroke: GRAY, PRIMROSE, RIDLEY.

Peterhouse: LANGHAM, GISBORNE, HOLBROOK, PERNE, [BROOKS], BIRDWOOD, CHALMERS, GRAY, WARKWORTH, [BEAUMONT], AINSWORTH.

Queens': [ERASMUS].

St Catharine's: HOADLY, SHERLOCK, EACHARD, WOODLARK, SHIRLEY, [RAMSDEN].

St John's: GILBERT, ASCHAM, METCALFE, GURNEY, COURTNEY, CLARKSON, WILBERFORCE, SYLVESTER, ADAMS, HERSCHEL, BATESON, HAVI-LAND, COCKCROFT, LADY MARGARET, BENIANS, SELWYN, VERULAM, [FAIRFAX].

Sidney Sussex: CROMWELL.

Trinity: NEWTON, BENTLEY, PORSON, RAYLEIGH, RUTHERFORD, [DIAMOND], MAITLAND, CAVENDISH, ZETLAND, SIDGWICK, SEDGWICK, SEDLEY TAYLOR, LUARD, ACTON, ADRIAN, BYRON, CLARENDON, [MELBOURNE], CLERK MAXWELL, MANSEL, DALTON, LANSDOWNE.

Trinity Hall: BATEMAN, CHESTERFIELD, WARREN, THIRLEBY, WOODHEAD, FRASER, LATHAM, GELDART.

All these provide certainty about explanations of street-names. The clusters of names of High Stewards and of military men also leave no doubt. It is a fairly safe bet that most of the mayors have been honoured, several in the area around

CAMPKIN Road, along with some local people. Few university names are in this part of Cambridge. Unusual names with a local connection offer some probability. Groups of Roman (MINERVA, etc.) and Anglo-Saxon names (QUEEN EDITH, etc.) offer complete certainty.

In other clusters some historical association may be at least strongly inviting, as with [MELBOURNE], CLARENDON, VICTORIA and EARL, and the fact that the two first named were both at Trinity at almost the same time strengthens the case. BURLEIGH and JAMES together are a good pointer to the man named in NORFOLK Street, James Burleigh's father-in-law. GEORGE IV, REGENT, CAROLINE, CORONA-TION, BENTINCK and in another cluster the various streets named BRUNSWICK shed light on one another. Geographical clusters are found in BRENTWOOD, CHIGWELL, COGGESHALL, THE RODINGS, TIPTREE, all in Essex (with BERGHOLT, in Suffolk, but near the other villages) and EDINBURGH, DUNDEE, INVERNESS, KINROSS, STIR-LING, all in the area once occupied by SCOTLAND Farm (where Scottish cattle halted on the way to London?).

Where problems arise, several criteria can be used, not necessarily to provide certainty. Sometimes, but rarely, the name is recorded in Council Minutes as suggested by a college or an individual. Where there is more than one choice, a close connection with Cambridge is a strong indication. A pair of names like AYLESTONE and HUMBERSTONE, for streets close to one another and built at about the same time, suggests a connection with Leicester, since both are parts of that city. But [BULSTRODE] and [HEDGERLEY], parallel with one another, although both are names of villages in Buckinghamshire, may refer to people. Lord William (Henry

Cavendish) Bentinck, later governor-general of India, was born at Bulstrode in 1774, and Sir Richard Bulstrode, educated at Pembroke Hall, a well-known royalist in the Civil War, whose father was Edward Bulstrode of Hedgerley, seemed a likely candidate until Mr Wise pointed out to us that Christopher Stone Bulstrode (1818–94) owned a house called 'Hedgerley House' on the site of the present street of that name. He was a cabinet-maker and upholsterer with premises opposite Trinity College Chapel, and was a trustee of Hobson's Conduit in 1868, so evidently a man of some consequence in the town. Both names could be connected in more than the place-names, but there is no conclusive evidence.

Proximity is another criterion: there can be no other IZAAK WALTON or Steve FAIRBAIRN, and these connect, being near the river, with ANGLERS Way, LENTS, MAYS, GRAYLING and LONG REACH (which might puzzle a total stranger, connecting it with boxing, rather than a stretch of the Cam).

Builders and developers are to be inferred because their names are often well known in Cambridge, like KELSEY and KERRIDGE, whose association nobody living in Cambridge could doubt. Spalding's and Kelly's Cambridge directories often list names of shopkeepers and tradesmen.

We aim at certainty, but have included, in brackets, some names that are reasonably well connected, or simply interesting. The main object of writing about street-names is after all not to trace exactly every single case, though the effort at exactness has to be made, but also to connect the names in such a way as will make the past of Cambridge come alive. In any historical account we look back over hundreds of years, but with street-names there is a daily reminder of some particular person or event. So one of the medieval fields round Cambridge, BRAD-MORE, comes to mind, and the Anglo-Saxon lands at Cherry Hinton owned by QUEEN EDITH and her relatives, and the farms at UPHALL and NETHERHALL, like HALL FARM, MANOR Farm, ELFLEDA Farm and GRANGE Road, which constitute a ring of formerly open spaces round the present built-up area. The city grows from its two small centres on CASTLE Street and near St BENET's church – where very few medieval names now survive – as it takes in the new population along MILL Road brought by the railways. CHESTERTON, once separate, links up, and so does BARNWELL. Windmills appear in the mind's eye at FRENCH'S Road and MILL Street, and theatres, hospitals for lepers, prisons occupy spaces that now look dull by comparison. The romantic atmosphere of Cambridge, its main attraction for tourists, is tempered by the awareness through street-names that the Backs were in medieval times a long harbour for barges coming up from King's Lynn or Wisbech, and that even in the nineteenth century coal and corn were passing all the time under the ancient bridges and past the architectural wonders. On the site of St John's Master's Lodge was once an iron foundry; the river-bank up to Newnham mill was crowded with men unloading barges and tending the horses that had brought them there; there was even a foundry by Market Hill. There have been breweries in Magdalene Street and Trinity Street, a malting-house during the late nineteenth century in the school of Pythagoras (Merton Hall), a coprolite mine on the site of New Hall, gravel pits in East Road, a military hospital where the University Library is, a steam-plough works in Cherry Hinton – all seeming now encroachments in residential areas or college precincts.

A book of this size can only suggest, so to speak, avenues to be explored. For this reason a large number of books and pamphlets on Cambridge history are included, and not in a separate bibliography, but immediately after the mention of some individual or aspect that arouses special interest. There is much more, too, in P. H. Reaney's *The Place-Names of Cambridgeshire and the Isle of Ely*, 1943, in the English Place-Names Society's Series, in the many volumes of the Dictionary of National Biography, of the Victoria County History of Cambridgeshire, Charles Henry Cooper's *Annals*, 1842–52, and the reports of the Royal Commission on Historical Monuments, as well as in Nikolaus Pevsner's volume, *Cambridgeshire*, 1954, in the Buildings of England series, and R. Willis and J. W. Clark's monumental *Architectural History of the University of Cambridge* (which also includes gardens). Sara Payne's articles in the *Cambridge Evening News*, published in two volumes as *Down Your Street*, 1983 and 1984, are also valuable. The Cambridgeshire Collection in the Central Library building in Lion Yard has newspapers, maps, photographs, books, pamphlets, card-indexes in profusion. The maps of Inclosures in the County Record Office provide many useful indications. May this brief account lead to greater enjoyment of all these, and may readers go on to interpret the significance of street-names further.

Spellings in maps and in the streets themselves are not always reliable. The name of MARTIN'S STILE LANE appears on the street-sign without an apostrophe 's', seeming to make Stile a surname. [MANERS], shown thus on the street-sign, appears on one map as [MANNERS], perhaps appropriately, since the latter is a family name of the Dukes of RUTLAND. GODESDONE has been the name on the street-sign for many years, though the original name was Godesone. [AUGERS] Road in Cherry

Hinton looks suspiciously like a mis-spelling of Aungers, the name of a family which owned land at the other end of Cambridge, near High Cross, and at Coton. (It appears in the index of the *Local Red Book* map as Algiers, but correctly on the map itself.) The surname Augers does, however, exist, and the Aingers family were large landowners in Histon. (See Clive Ennals, *Street Names in Histon and Impington*, 1985) On one map AKEMAN appears incorrectly as Axeman. Stainsfield appears in the *Local Red Book* map instead of STANESFIELD. KELSEY appears as Kesley in the same map, which also has Packenham for PAKENHAM, and ST BARNABUS as well as other mishaps. Lingrey appears to have been put sometimes for LINGEY, being not far from Lingey Fen, so spelt, correctly, on the Ordnance Survey and A–Z maps, though Barnett has Lingrey for both. [WILKIN] should perhaps be Wilkins, for the reason given below (p. 84). We have interpreted with a little freedom where doubts caused by these and other instances occur.

Nearly all the printed works mentioned can be consulted in the Cambridgeshire Collection.

Magdalene Street

Prehistoric

The only street-name in Cambridge that has connections with prehistoric times is ARBURY Road. The name is spelled Herburg, Ertburg, and similarly in thirteenth-century documents, and means earthwork. It used to be thought that Arbury Camp, at the north end of the road, was a fort like the one at Wandlebury or the War Ditches on LIME KILN Hill, south of the reservoir (now destroyed), but it is today regarded as an undefended site. A low circular bank and ditch about 100 metres in diameter, it was almost certainly an Iron Age enclosure for keeping animals safe from wolves and robbers. (See Alison Taylor, *Prehistoric Cambridgeshire*, 1977, and Sallie Purkis, *Arbury Is Where We Live*, EARO, The Resource Centre, Back Hill, Ely, 1981.)

Roman

In the late first century BCE Catuvellaunian settlers created a village on the spur of CASTLE hill. This was abandoned at the time of the Roman conquest, and between 43 BCE and 70 CE the Romans built a military camp there. The Catuvellaunians may have taken part in the rebellion of Boadicea after 60 CE, or have suffered for it. The Romans were not there to tolerate insubordination. (See David J. Breeze, *Roman Forts in Britain*, 1994.)

The Roman 'castrum' was bounded on two sides by the line of MOUNT PLEASANT, where there was a wall and a ditch. This turned at a right angle and probably continued across HUNTINGDON Road to CLARE Street and back down the line of MAGRATH Avenue to near CHESTERTON Lane, turning to the south-west through KETTLE'S YARD and then north-west up HONEY HILL. The last of these is a name often found, making a rustic joke about a particularly muddy place, not much like honey. However, local residents prefer the name Pooh Corner, alluding to the great bear's favourite relish. Kettle was a former owner. (See David M. Browne, *Roman Cambridgeshire*, 1977; also Mac Dowdy, *Romans in the Cambridge Area*, Cambridge Antiquarian Society, Excavation at Shire Hall, 1983.)

A gate to the Roman camp was slightly to the north-west of ALBION Row. Here the legions marched in to their barracks.

CHESTERTON Lane derives its name from 'ceastre', originally the Roman camp or 'castrum'. (Chesterton was for many centuries separate administratively from Cambridge, as is implied by the Victoria Bridge, which has the Cambridge arms on the south side, and the equivalent for Chesterton on the north. It included the medieval castle.) A Roman road from Ermine Street near Wimpole passed through Barton and continued north-east of the camp. It is called AKEMAN Street, but the street that now has this name is at right angles to the original one, which followed almost exactly the line of STRETTEN (sometimes spelled STRETTON) Avenue, evidently named after a Chief Constable of Cambridgeshire (Charles James Derrickson Stretten, born in 1830, who was connected with St LUKE'S Church, near his HQ, as were several others such as those named in HALE and SEARLE Street, and HARVEY

GOODWIN Avenue. Less likely is the first Master of Trinity Hall, Robert Stretton, who resigned in 1355.) At CARLTON Way the line of the Roman road is followed exactly; the name is that of Henry Boyle, first Lord Carlton, who died in 1725, was MP for Cambridge University 1692–1705 and Chancellor of the Exchequer in 1701. His coat-of-arms appeared on the inn-sign of the Carlton Arms until 1996.

Akeman Street continues in MERE Way, near the city boundary – 'mere' being a name often used for a boundary or division – and then in a straight line, becoming a track up which the legions marched towards Ely; beyond there the road led to Denver and the coast at Brancaster. 'Akeman' was derived by antiquarians, without justification, from 'Acemanes-ceastre', an ancient name for Bath.

The course of the Roman road from the south is now marked by the part of HILLS Road beginning at STATION Road, continuing in REGENT Street, ST ANDREW'S Street, SIDNEY Street, BRIDGE Street, MAGDALENE Street, CASTLE Street and HUNTINGDON Road. (From STATION Road southwards the old road diverges slightly until WORTS' Causeway.) It is often called the Via Devana, but this is again a name mistakenly given by antiquarians who believed it was part of a road that led from Colchester to Chester.

A recent cluster of street-names straddling the course of the Roman road beyond MERE Way is devoted to Roman mythology and history. AUGUSTUS Close is named after the Roman Emperor (63 BCE–14 CE), APOLLO Way after the Roman god of the sun, NEPTUNE Close after the god of the sea, MINERVA Way after the goddess of wisdom and of arts and trades, who was also the goddess of war. HERCULES Close is named after the fantastically strong hero who was proclaimed a god after his death. A bronze statuette of him has been found at Sutton-in-the-Isle. (See Miranda J. Green, *The Gods of Roman Britain*, 1994.) All these names would have been familiar to the occupants of the Roman villa, remains of which have been found in an area around FORTESCUE Road and HUMPHREYS Road. It was L-shaped and had three or four rooms, with a pottery kiln and cemetery. The 'courts' (not streets) in this area include Roman, Villa, Portico, Pavilion, Forum, Temple, Emperor, Tribune, Consul, Legion and Legate, all with Roman connections.

Anglo-Saxon

When the Romans left Cambridge, their buildings were not preserved by the Angles, Jutes and Saxons, some of whom began to arrive in the late fourth century. For hundreds of years there were raids and pillagings, especially by the Danes.

In the seventh century, according to ST BEDE (673–735), the historian of the English church and people, there was 'a little ruined city called Grantchester [i.e. Cambridge]', where monks discovered a stone coffin to enshrine the bones of St Etheldreda, who had founded Ely Cathedral. (There is a window showing St Bede in Holy Sepulchre Church.) But despite the raids and battles, by the time of Domesday Book nearly all the present day villages were in existence, and Cambridge had a church dating from *c.* 1020, possibly founded by King Canute. (See Alison Taylor, *Anglo-Saxon Cambridge*, 1978.)

The names CAMBRIDGE and CAM appear in several street-names. 'Camboritum' was never the name of the city but 'Durolipons' is now suggested by historians as well as 'Durcinate' (or 'Curcinate') and the rather ugly 'Durovigutum'. In Bede's day it was Grantacaestir, and similar names occur until 1170. In 875 'three Danes' wintered in Grantebrygge, selecting it apparently as a place of some importance. Three great ships with oars, coming along the course of the rowing races, are still visible to the mind's eye. In about 945 the name Grontabricc occurs, and similar names continue until 1187. In 1086 Cantebrigie appears, continuing in similar forms till 1454. Caumbrig(g)e appears in 1348, and variants of this lead on to the modern form. Thus 'the Roman fort (–caestir) on the Granta' is later 'the bridge over the Granta (i.e. 'muddy river')'. The 'r' was lost, and the 'G' became 'C', says Reaney, 'because of the inevitable difficulties of the Frenchman [i.e. Norman] in pronouncing a succession of liquids'. (See Reaney, *The Place-Names of Cambridgeshire and the Isle of Ely*.) Otherwise Cambridge would be Grambridge, but none the worse for that.

There is a SAXON Street, and a SAXON Road, the latter being near to the supposed hut of the Saxon hermit Godesone (God's son), remembered in the mis-spelt GODESDONE Road. Near a holy well going back to pagan times he had a wooden oratory dedicated to St Andrew, to whom the church on Newmarket Road is consecrated. (Another hermit sat by the bridge where SILVER Street bridge now is, collecting tolls, as hermits often did, many being no more men of religion than eighteenth-century toll-keepers were, but the name is unexplained. There are many Silver Streets, and as Reaney says they cannot all have been occupied by silversmiths – but surely a place like Cambridge needed them?) SAXON *Street* was once part of an 'architectural' trio including also Gothic and Doric Streets; the latter have both disappeared.

To the south-west, a cluster of Anglo-Saxon names is due to Council policy in recent years, of naming streets after the former owners of land in the neighbourhood. The policy was advocated by the mayor, Howard MALLETT, whose name appears in the name of a manor at Hinton, dating from Norman times. The former Youth Club opposite Young Street is named after both. QUEEN EDITH'S Way remembers Editha, consort of Edward the Confessor (*c.* 1003–66), who married her in 1045. She was the owner of the manor of Hinton, now Cherry Hinton, and daughter of Earl Godwin, remembered in GODWIN Way and GODWIN Close.

This Godwin, Earl of the West Saxons, died in 1053. He was probably the son of the South Saxon Wulfnoth, but according to later stories he was the son of a churl. In 1042 he helped to raise to the throne Edward the Confessor, the last Anglo-Saxon king of the old line, and elder son of Ethelred the Unready. Godwin led the opposition to Edward's foreign favourites, and Edward revenged himself by insulting Queen Edith, confining her to a monastery and banishing Godwin and his sons. They returned to England in 1052 and forced the King to agree to Godwin's demands.

Godwin's son was Harold, whom William the Conqueror defeated at Hastings in 1066.

Also remembered here, in GUNHILD Close, Court and Way, is the daughter of King Canute, who succeeded Ethelred the Unready, after defeating Edmund Ironside.

The proposal to name a street after Wulfnoth, probably Godwin's father, was dropped because of the difficulty of pronouncing it. [WULFSTAN] Way was named instead, possibly after St Wulfstan, a Bishop of Worcester (*c.* 1009–95), reputed author of part of the *Anglo-Saxon Chronicle*, who is said to have put an end to the slave trade at Bristol. He was canonised in 1203. There is a translation by J. H. F. Peile, published 1934, of his *Life*. The alternative is Wulfstan (d. 1023) who was Archbishop of York, and author of many Old English homilies, treatises and law codes. He had some connection with Fenland abbeys. His influence brought Canute to Christianity, and thereby saved Anglo-Saxon civilisation from disaster.

ELFLEDA Road commemorates a great Saxon benefactress whose husband, Ealdorman Bryhtnoth, was killed fighting against the Danes in 991. A window in the parish church of Ely is dedicated to him. (See 'The Battle of Maldon', the greatest of all late Old English poems.) There was an Elfleda Farm in this area in 1920.

BENE'T Street is named after St Benedict (480–?543), the founder of Western monasticism. The church, formerly serving as the chapel of Corpus Christi College, also bears his name, as did the college for some 350 years after its foundation in 1352. The church still has an Anglo-Saxon tower and chancel arch, and gives grounds for thinking that before the Conquest a community lived here, as well as the one around Castle Hill.

DITTON Fields, Lane and Walk, like the village of Fen Ditton, derive their names from Anglo-Saxon 'tūn by the dūc', i.e. the farm by the dyke, Fleam Dyke, originally called simply 'ditch' ('Flem Ditch' in local speech), as in HIGH DITCH Road. 'Fleam' seems to have meant 'Ditch of Refuge', from the Old English word *fleam* meaning 'flight'. This road is at the end of the Dyke, a rampart stretching across to Balsham via Fulbourn, which is one of five parallel ramparts, blocking passage between the river and the uplands; the largest is the Devil's Dyke, from Reach to Newmarket, dating from late

Roman times. Locally the pasque flower that used to grow on Fleam Dyke was known as 'Dane's Blood'. There was a battle with the Danes at the Balsham end.

Medieval

Cambridge grew out of two settlements, divided by the river. CASTLE Street runs through the northern one. (See H. C. Darby, *Medieval Cambridgeshire*.) The castle itself was built by order of William the Conqueror in 1068, and was of the motte and bailey type, the still existing mound being the motte, and the area north-west of this forming the bailey. (See Alison Taylor, *Castles of Cambridgeshire*, Cambridgeshire County Council, no date, and W. M. Palmer, *Cambridge Castle*, 1928.) The area was known as 'the Borough'; its male inhabitants were 'the Borough Boys'. Here ST PETER'S Street runs past the small St Peter's Church, sometimes compared to the one in Samuel Palmer's *The Magic Apple Tree* in the Fitzwilliam Museum. Roman bricks from the Roman camp can still be seen round the doorway. POUND Hill was near the former Pound Green, where straying animals were impounded by the pindar. (There was another pound in the middle of FAIR Street by Midsummer Common and one at the Cattle Market.) HAYMARKET Road was conveniently near the pound. (For MOUNT PLEASANT and HONEY HILL see the Roman section.) LADY MARGARET Road is named after the mother of Henry VII, Lady Margaret Beaufort, who founded St John's College, on whose land the road lies. (ST JOHN'S Place is off CASTLE Street.) ALBION Row and ALBION Yard relate to an ancient name for England. In legend Albion was a giant, son of Neptune, who first discovered the island and ruled over it for forty-four years, or alternatively, in legend, he was the first Christian martyr, who left his name to the country. [SHELLY] Row was Shallow Row in the 1830s, and is almost always spelled without a second 'e'. One explanation is that many oyster shells, supposedly discarded by Roman soldiers, and found in gardens there, gave rise to the name. (See Enid Porter, 'The Castle End of Cambridge', *Cambridgeshire and Peterborough Life*, November 1970, pp. 20–2.)

The 'Borough' scarcely grew in size between Roman times and the late nineteenth century. The centre of Cambridge shifted to south of the bridge. (See Arthur Gray, *The Town of Cambridge*, 1925.)

The existence of a bridge is indicated by the name 'Grontabricc' in about 945, but a wooden bridge is said to have been made between 673 and 875, possibly built by Offa, King of Mercia (d. 796), the southern boundary of whose kingdom lay along the north bank of the river, while Offa's Dyke, its western boundary, runs along the border of Wales and England. That there were Danes south of the bridge is indicated by the dedication of ST CLEMENT'S Church: the saint was popular with the Danes. (Cf. St Clement Danes in London.) BRIDGE Street was called Briggestrate in 1254. In 1276 the Sheriff levied sums for the repair of the bridge, but kept most of the money for himself, as well as money charged for the use of a barge which he provided. The keeper of the Sheriff's prison was accused of removing planks from the bridge by night, to delay repairs and augment the Sheriff's profits. In medieval times there was a ducking-chair for 'scolds' at the middle of the bridge. One made in 1745 was in need of replacement in 1766. (See J. H. Bullock, 'Bridge Street, Cambridge: Notes and Memories', *Cambridge*

Public Library Record, 11 (1939), pp. 11–23, 47–60, 110–19, and Enid Porter, 'Bridge Street, Cambridge, in the Last Century', *Cambridgeshire and Peterborough Life*, April 1970, pp. 24–6.) The last wooden bridge was replaced in 1756 by a stone bridge designed by James ESSEX. In 1799 this was declared ruinous; it was replaced by the present cast-iron, Magdalene bridge, completed in 1823. (See Richard J. Pierpoint, *Cam Bridges*, 1976.)

QUAYSIDE was in use in the twelfth century, when Henry I instituted a law prohibiting the unloading of any goods on the seaward side of Cambridge. This increased the importance of the town considerably.

ROUND CHURCH Street runs beside the Church of the Holy Sepulchre. The oldest part, built in 1130–40, is circular in imitation of the Holy Sepulchre in Jerusalem, known to Crusaders. It was severely restored in 1841. Opposite the church is the apex of a triangle reaching to ALL SAINTS Passage, the present name referring to the Church of All Saints in the Jewry, destroyed in 1865 and rebuilt in Jesus Lane. The older name was 'Vico Judaeorum', or 'Pilats Lane', marking the base of the triangle containing the Jewry. The Jewry was pillaged, and on 12 August 1266, despite letters patent of April ordering there should be no molestation, many Jews were murdered. Robert Pecche, or BECHE, was one of the murderers, who attacked and plundered non-Jews also. In 1275 all remaining Jews were deported en masse to Huntingdon, to satisfy the demand of Queen Eleanor, widow of Henry III, that no Jew should be allowed in any town she held in dower. A stone house belonging to Benjamin the Jew, a landowner, near the west corner of the present Guildhall was later in use as a town gaol. Jews were expelled from England in 1291.

10

The largest part of the medieval town was bounded on the north and west by the river, and on the south and east by the King's Ditch, the course of which ran along MILL Lane, then PEMBROKE Street (formerly Langrithe Lane, the lane of the long channel), across the Crowne Plaza site to POST OFFICE Terrace, then past the Barnwell Gate up HOBSON Street, through the grounds of Sidney Sussex College and along PARK Street to the river. It is first referred to in 1268, as a means of keeping the town cleansed of dirt and filth, but its origin is much earlier. In fact it was used as a dump for entrails, dung and garbage. Privies were built over it, and for centuries sanitation remained poor. In 1574 it was said to be a cause of the plague but not until the nineteenth century was it completely covered over.

Within these bounds lay PETTY CURY, called 'parva Cokeria' in 1330, 'le Petitecurye' in 1344, and similarly in later times. It has been thought that part of MARKET Hill may have been called the Cury or Cooks' Row, and that this street was called the Petty Cury to distinguish it from the larger one. In 1972 the south side was demolished; the loss of so many old buildings, to be replaced by complete uniformity, was a disaster for Cambridge. (See Henry Bosanquet, *Walks Round Vanished Cambridge. Petty Cury*, Cambridge History Agency, 1974, and Enid Porter, 'Petty Cury', *Cambridgeshire and Peterborough Life*, June 1970, pp. 24–6.)

Many street-names of medieval times have not survived so well. CORN EXCHANGE Street, for instance, was le Feireyerd Lane (i.e. Fair Lane) in 1495, and Slaughter House Lane in 1596 and 1798. DRUMMER Street was Drusemere in *c.* 1248, probably meaning 'muddy pool': the shape of the present bus-station there is still pool-like. FREE SCHOOL Lane had many names suggesting 'muddy stream'; MARKET

Street is Cordewanaria in 1322, referring to cordwainers who worked in Cordovan leather, and other products were sold in le Chesemarketh, le Maltmarket, and Botry rowe, le Duddery (where woollen cloth or clothes were sold), Milk Market, Cutlers' Row, Lorimers' Row ('Lorimer' means 'maker of metal harness'), Smearmongers' Row (for tallow, lard and grease), Pewterers' Row and 'The Shraggery' for old clothes. PEAS Hill is a hill only in Cambridge terms, though it once stood on a slope leading down to the river, and it may never have seen a pea. It was a fish-market in living memory and for centuries before that – 'peas' may be a corruption of Latin *pisces*, a fish. A market for peas only sounds unlikely. (See Enid Porter, 'Cambridge Market Place', *Cambridgeshire and Peterborough Life*, December 1969, pp. 24–6.) Parallel to GUILDHALL Street, where Fisher Hall is, was Sparrow Lane. The site of the Crowne Plaza was the Hog Market; a Hog Market Fair was held here on 'Hog *Hill*' – yet another case of *lucus a non lucendo*. DOWNING Street was, until the college was founded, Bird-Bolt (i.e. crossbow-arrow) Lane, earlier Dowdewerslane, corrupted from Deus Deners, itself corrupted from Duzedeners, 'twelve-penny', the name of a family. Almost every street in the medieval town had a different name from the one now used, and some have no relation to any modern street, like Creepers' Lane and 'Le Endelesweye', so called because 'yt nether haeth beginnyng nor endynge'. (Similar 'endless ways' exist in other towns.)

GARRET HOSTEL Lane is named after a former student hostel, which may have had a watch-tower or garret overlooking the entrance to the town by the Garret Hostel bridge. (See H. P. Stokes, *The Medieval Hostels of the University of Cambridge*, Cambridge Antiquarian Society Octavo Publications, no. 44, 1924.)

One 'lost' name is Milne Street, which ran from the QUEENS' Lane of today across what are now the grounds of King's College, through the site of King's College Chapel and so to TRINITY Lane. This led to the hithes along the river-bank, where salt, coal, flax, corn and other commodities were unloaded, but lost value as a street when the chapel was built across it. The present MILL Lane, however, led to the King's Mill and Bishop's Mill, of which the weir and mill-pond remain. These date back to the time soon after the Conquest, when Picot the sheriff, co-founder of BARNWELL Priory, built them or at least one of them. (MILL *Road* is named after a windmill that stood at the corner of COVENT GARDEN, remembered par-ticularly in MILL Street. MILL Way in Grantchester refers to a mill belonging to the NUTTERS family.)

The mill at TRUMPINGTON (formerly Trumpintune, Tromphintonam, i.e. Trump's Farm, perhaps from Gothic *trumpe*, a 'surly person') was made famous by CHAUCER (*c.* 1345–1400) through the Reeve's Tale in the *Canterbury Tales*, designed about 1387, beginning:

> At Trumpingtoun, nat fer fro Cantebrigge,
> Ther gooth a brok, and over that a brigge,
> Upon the whiche brook ther stant a melle;
> And this is verray sooth that I yow telle.

The tale is about two 'clerks' – students – who are cheated by a miller out of part of their meal, and revenge themselves on him by going to bed with his wife and daughter. The mill in question, according to the Chaucer scholar W.W. Skeat, was probably slightly south-west of the village, by the Old Mill Holt beside the river.

ST BOTOLPH'S Church, named after an East Anglian saint,

stands near the old Trumpington gate; travellers would make their prayers there before setting off or returning, as he was generally regarded as their protector.

DE FREVILLE Avenue bears the name of a Norman family whose tombs are in Little Shelford Church. The estate was bought by Edward Humphrey Green who claimed descent from them on his wife's side. Arthur Gray tells a story in his *Tedious Brief Tales* – no doubt an invented one – of a priest, Sir Nicholas de Frevile, who was dying of the Black Death, and was helped by a nun from St Radegund's convent who at his death left a white rose on his breast. According to Sara Payne a white ('Iceberg') rose was planted in St Peter's churchyard in recent times, to remember them both: a nice instance of fiction becoming reality. In Great Shelford there is a de Freville Arms, built about 1850, and a de Freville farm, part of the house dating from *c.* 1500, being probably part of a vanished medieval hall. (See *From Domesday to Dormitory. The History of the Landscape of Great Shelford*, duplicated typescript.)

Granham's Manor Farm in Great Shelford, to which GRANHAM's Road leads, is to be associated with John de Grendon or de Crendon (1355), variously spelt Grandames (1535), Graundehams (1553), Grandhams (1597). For the interchange of Gr- and Cr- see p. 4 above under CAMBRIDGE. Granham's Camp is probably an ancient earthworks.

A leper hospital founded in 1361 by Henry de Tangmere and dedicated to ST ANTHONY and ST ELIGIUS is commemorated in two streets. Later, almshouses named after the saints stood on and in front of the sites of nos. 6 and 7 Trumpington Street. They were pulled down in 1852 and rebuilt in Panton Street, from which a statue of St Anthony with his emblems, a pig and a bell, is visible. St Eligius was the patron saint of goldsmiths and blacksmiths. Legend relates how he shoed a recalcitrant horse, as in the clerihew:

> St Eligius
> Was rather religious.
> He cut the leg off a horse
> But stuck it back, of course.

(See D. Haigh, *The Religious Houses of Cambridgeshire*, Cambridgeshire County Council, 1988.) There is a wall-painting of this miracle in the church at Slapton, Northamptonshire, and a similar miracle, by St Anthony, is illustrated both by Titian and Donatello.

Outside the town precincts, before the nineteenth-century Inclosures, the fields on the east side were known as Barnwell Field, and those on the west as Cambridge Field. Each was cultivated on the three-field system, Barnwell Field being divided into Middle Field, Ford Field and Brademere Field, after which BRADMORE Lane and Street off East Road were named in Victorian times. The name means 'broad mere'.

Each of these fields was divided into furlongs (the length of a furrow, whatever that might be); each furlong had its own name, as in ORWELL FURLONG, and was divided into strips. Villagers owned pieces of such strips in various furlongs, not close together, but allocated in order to give a fair distribution of better and poorer soil. These many unconnected and uneconomical strips were abolished (see 'Inclosures', pp. 118–21) and some owners to some extent compensated.

Another sign of agricultural history is WADLOES Road, named after Wadloes Footpath leading to Fen Ditton: this is derived from such names as Whatelowe and Watloe, probably meaning 'wheat-hill', but as usual in Cambridge street-names there is little sign of any hill.

Though the King's Ditch was a disaster, clean water was brought to the town by the Franciscans in 1325. CONDUIT HEAD Road is where their conduit began. It took the water by underground pipes passing *under* the river to the site of their monastery, now occupied by Sidney Sussex College. In 1546 the pipes were used to feed the fountain in Trinity Great Court, the only remaining place where the water is used. BRADBRUSHE Fields, leading from Conduit Head Road, is a recent street-name for a place called Branderusche and Bradrushe in the fourteenth century. (The name means 'burnt rushes' or 'broad place covered with rushes'.) It leads to Trinity Conduit Head. 'Bradderussh' is a tributary water course of the Girton WASHPIT brook, so called from the village sheep-dip. (See Catherine P. Hall and J. R. Ravensdale, eds., *The West Fields of Cambridge*, Cambridge Antiquarian Records Society, vol. 3, 1976.)

An old tradition is preserved in LAMMAS Field, and the adjoining Lammas Lane. 'Lammas' is a generic name for a kind of field, where the owner allowed common pasturage rights after 1 August (by which time his crops would have been harvested). The land opposite Darwin College, while owned by the Darwin family, was a Lammas land, and there were other such lands in Cambridge. (The name comes from *hlaf* (a loaf) and *maesse* (mass); in the early English church 1 August was a harvest festival, at which loaves of bread were consecrated, made from the first ripe corn.) The present Lammas land is by the paddling pool at Newnham.

Fields were often called 'leys' (leas), a name preserved in LEYS Avenue and LEYS Road, where there was a Leys Laundry in 1904, and in the Leys School on Trumpington Road.

Also outside the medieval centre is FAIR Street, named after Midsummer Fair, still held annually, but originally a commercial fair authorised by King John in 1212. STOURBRIDGE Grove commemorates the fair formerly held on Stourbridge Common, also authorised by John and dating from about 1211. The fair was proclaimed for the last time in 1933 by the mayor, Mrs Keynes, 'in the presence of a couple of women with babies in their arms and an ice-cream barrow'. It had been one of the great fairs of Europe and was the basis for Bunyan's Vanity Fair, in *Pilgrim's Progress*. Daniel Defoe in his *Tour*, written in the eighteenth century, described it much as it must have been in medieval times. The fairs at Leipzig, Frankfurt am Main, Nuremberg and Augsburg, he said, could not be compared. There were goldsmiths, toymen, brasiers, turners, 'milaners', haberdashers, hatters, mercers, drapers, pewterers and china-ware-houses, with tented coffee-houses, taverns and eating-houses. Mercery goods of all sorts were specially present, which gives rise to the name of the recent MERCERS' Row off Newmarket Road. Older names, post-medieval, registering particular commodities are GARLIC Row, CHEDDARS Lane and OYSTER Row; Oyster House, now demolished, was where oysters could be consumed, especially at the opening of the fair by the mayor and councillors. It was the centre of administration for the fair. In 1450-1 the nuns of ST RADE-GUND'S bought fish and timbers, pepper, soap and a churn. In 1549 ale and wine, bread, fish, flax, yarn, woollen and linen cloth, silk, pitch, tar, coal, charcoal, faggots, salt, hay and grain are mentioned. (See E. Coneybeare, *A History of Cambridgeshire*, 1897.)

The name Stourbridge is said to have probably meant originally 'steer-bridge', or 'ox-bridge', and not to have come from the river Stour which flows from Cherry Hinton Hall. It may be that oxen crossing the bridge were charged for.

Two ancient farms are remembered in NETHERHALL Way (the name is recorded in 1372) and UPHALL Road (1382). [BOWERS CROFT] is presumably the name of a croft belonging to an unidentified Bower in the area of Netherhall Farm. The manor of Hinton-Netherhall became the property of the Moubray family in the reign of Richard II. Thomas MOWBRAY (1366?–99) aided Richard in his wars against the Scots and Irish, arrested the King's enemies, and appears to have served him well, but was banished in 1398, and his estates forfeited to the Berkeleys. (An earlier owner of the manor was QUEEN EDITH.) In Shakespeare's play *Richard II*, Thomas Mowbray, Duke of Norfolk, is about to fight a duel with Bolingbroke when the King abruptly calls it off, and banishes both men, Bolingbroke for six years, Mowbray for life.

In 1501–2 Anne, Dowager Lady SCROOPE of Bolton bequeathed the manor of Newnham to GONVILLE Hall, now Gonville and Caius College. It had belonged to Roger MOR-TIMER, Kt, and she had to submit to a series of hard bargains with the Corporation of 1500, as she was both an absentee owner and a woman. In later years the Corporation still claimed the lordship of the manor, to the distress of Gonville Hall. The headquarters of the Mortimer Manor was a house somewhere in the garden of the present Newnham House and Ashton House, or possibly just in the Caius Fellows' Garden; it still appears on Hamond's map of 1592. The land lay in fact rather along the Backs, as they now are, than in Newnham. It included also the area of the present Scroope Terrace. (See Hall and Ravensdale, eds., *The West Fields of Cambridge*, p. 12, which also contains a chapter on 'The Genesis of the Backs'.)

COLDHAM'S Grove, Lane and Road have a name from medieval times, but the meaning was 'a cold hamlet', and the apostrophe was added later, suggesting a person, who never existed.

[GREEN END] is in an area that belonged to Nicholas Attegrene in 1279. [GREEN PARK] and [GREEN END] Road may also be named after him, but not GREEN Street or GREEN'S Road (see 'Inclosures', pp. 118–21). Attegrene owned part of the West Fields also. However, 'Green End' may merely refer to the end of Chesterton, as the same name refers to the end of Fen Ditton. The same name appears in Comberton, Cottenham and Long Stanton.

HOWES is the name of a hamlet, so called by 1279, either from the nearby barrow or from the slight rise on which it stood. It was still inhabited in the late fourteenth century, but was not recorded as a hamlet after 1600. A chapel named for St James existed there, perhaps founded by the Trumpingtons, but by *c.* 1800 only one or two dwellings remained. There is still an open space called Howes Close, but the hamlet was on the other side of the road, in the area of the University Farm.

An interesting explanation of KING'S HEDGES is given by T. McK. Hughes (see *Cambridge Review*, vol. 18, 4 February 1897, pp. 201–2). The road is in the area of the ancient King's warren, or game preserve, where hedges would have been grown to channel the game, pursued by tenants, into places where they could be easily killed. 'We may recall', writes Hughes, 'the gay cavalcade watched from the Castle walls on its way to the King's Hunting Box near the hedges, the winding of the huntsman's horn, and the rush of deer and boar and many another creature that has long since vanished from our district.' The name is recorded in 1588 as Kinges Headge.

RED CROSS is marked as a cross and so named at the junction of WORTS' Causeway and Hills Road in the Cherry Hinton Inclosures map, although the cross is not included by Reaney in his account of Cambridge boundary crosses, of which this clearly is one. As you entered Cambridge you would always find a cross to comfort or warn you.

Barnwell

In 1092 Hugolina, wife of the Norman Sheriff Picot, fell ill. She vowed that if God would restore her to health she would found a monastery, and fortunately in three days she had recovered. Her husband built a church dedicated to St Giles, remains of which are still visible in the nineteenth-century church of that name, at the foot of CASTLE Street, where Picot held sway over the Anglo-Saxons. They claimed that he took from them common of pasture on which to build his mills. A monk of Ely, taking their side, called him 'a hungry lion, a ravening wolf, a filthy hog', while his son Robert was charged with conspiracy against the King in 1095, and fled. In 1108 the Augustinian canons moved to the site now occupied by the Old Abbey House in ABBEY Road. The church they built within the area between NEWMARKET Road, GODESDONE Road, PRIORY Road and ABBEY Road had cloisters, a chapter house, a frater and eventually a Lady Chapel; it was a very large construction, of which only a few stones and the so-called Cellarer's Chequer in Priory Road remain. The monastery was dissolved in 1539, and the present, charming old house built in its place. It is said to be haunted, of course. (See Florence A. Keynes, *By-ways of Cambridge History*, 1947, for the house and priory, and *Journal of the Society for Psychical Research*, vol. 46, no. 753 (Sept. 1972), pp. 109–23.)

PRIORY Road gives the correct name of BARNWELL Priory, this, rather than 'Abbey', being the usual title in Augustinian monasteries. The name meant 'children's well', or less probably 'warriors' well': young people wrestled and sang and played musical instruments on Midsummer Common, once called Grenecroft. (See Ena Mitchell, *Notes on the History of Four Cambridge Commons*, no date.)

The priors of Barnwell are recorded in the *Liber Memorandorum ecclesie de Bernwelle*, and their dates have been established by J. W. Clark (Publications of the Cambridge Antiquarian Society, vol. 33, 1933, pp. 247–9). Written in 1295–6, the accounts of each prior in the earlier years must rely on tradition, although a lost chronicle of the house may have been used. Of Geoffrey, or GALFRID (1092–1112), the first, we are told he 'died old and full of days in great sanctity'. Pain PEVEREL, who had been a standard-bearer in the Holy Land, began in 1112 a church 'of wondrous dimensions'; the first prior after this was GERARD (1112–53). But Pain Peverel's son William went on a crusade and died in 1148, leaving the church unfinished, until with the help of Everard de BECHE, Sheriff 1170–7, a principal benefactor, it was completed. Laurence de STANESFIELD (1238–51), the ninth prior, 'built the frater and the farmery, the great guest hall, the granary, the bakehouse and brewhouse, the stable for horses, the inner and outer gatehouse, and the walls of the new work almost to the top. He finished the chapel of St Edmund and covered it with lead.' These very extensive buildings have all disappeared. Laurence was at once ascetic and kindly, so devoted to observance that when no longer able to walk he would have himself carried to the entrance of the choir. Johanus de THORLEYE (1254–66), the eleventh prior, 'built a handsome chamber (perhaps the Cellarer's Chequer, but the name is only surmised) and a chapel for himself, and rebuilt the west pane of the cloister. He is described as a shrewd, hard little man, who took over a large debt. After the battle of Lewes he was on a visit to a manor belonging to Barnwell Priory at Wiggenhall, near King's Lynn. The attack on him and his party by brigands is related in the *Liber* with great vivacity: 'the aforesaid robbers took away all the Prior's horses and harness, leaving only one aged horse', and 'putting on the Canons' rain-copes, in derision of them and their order, made loud laughter and mockery'. Not long after, the fenmen burned Johanus's barns at Bourne, 'and some of the islanders conspired his death, upon account of Sir Walter de Cottenham, who was taken by the King's officers, and hanged'. Later, John de Burgh of Harston demanded the loan of a war-horse, but the only one the prior still had was the aged one the brigands had spared, whereupon John and his cronies 'came about the aforesaid horse, some showing its teeth, some feeling its head and back, some pricking it and making it kick. "Skin it", said some. "Burn it", said others.' At length Johanus fled to Waltham Abbey, fell ill and resigned. The priory was only saved by descendants of BECHE, who sided with the rebels.

John of Bourne (1345–50) was sixteenth prior, but [BOURNE] Road is not near the other streets named after priors and may have been meant for the village west of the city. The name of Richard de NORTON (1350–?), his successor, however, is in the cluster, as are the names of John BARNWELL (1392–1408), William RAYSON (1517) and Thomas RAWLYN (1523).

The cluster of 'Barnwell' streets above occupies most of the site of what was once Marshall's WHITEHILL Aerodrome, 1929–37.

Robert BARNES was prior not of Barnwell Priory but of the Augustinian friary in the middle of town, where the old Cavendish Laboratory later stood, from 1523 to 1525. (These friars were distinct from the Augustinian canons of Barnwell, who had a more missionary role.) Barnes had studied at Louvain and was attracted by the new doctrines of Luther, an Augustinian like himself. He joined other Austin friars and Miles Coverdale, translator of the Bible, at the Old Schools and at sermons in Great St Mary's. There were also meetings at a house called the White Horse, on the present border between King's and St Catharine's. Adversaries called it 'Little Germany'. Sermons given by Barnes in St Edward's Church, where LATIMER also preached, led to his being accused of heresy. He recanted, was imprisoned, escaped overseas but returned to England and was burned at the stake in 1540. (See E. Gordon Rupp, *The English Protestant Tradition*, 1947.)

In the early nineteenth century the whole site of the priory was covered with fragments of various dimensions, and slender round columns of Purbeck marble mingled with capitals and other architectural ornaments. A carved stone angel from the priory is still preserved in the Folk Museum.

Soon after Barnwell Priory, a Benedictine nunnery was founded, dedicated to St Mary, later to St Mary and ST RADEGUND, on Grenecroft, or Midsummer Common, now the site of JESUS College. The Common included what is now called Jesus Green. Here the nuns held a so-called garlic fair (see also p. 17), in the grounds of the present college – until *c.* 1830 PARK Street was called Garlic Fair Lane. (St Radegund

23

(518–87), born in Thuringia, was forced into marriage with the Frankish King Chlotar I, but left him after he murdered her brother, and established a nunnery at Poitiers. She formed a close friendship with the poet who wrote the famous hymn 'Vexilla regis'. Her *Life* was written by F. Brittain, a Fellow of Jesus, in 1925.) The nunnery was finally dissolved to make place for the college. It had been reduced to utter ruin by the incompetence, extravagance and dissolute life of the nuns, their moral decline being attributed to the proximity of the University.

Town and gown

The comparative luxury in which scholars lived, and their unaccountability in common law, gave rise to resentment in the town, although a law imposing maximum wages, and the losses caused by the Black Death also played a part. At the time of the Peasants' Revolt in 1381 the mayor and others burned the house of the University bedell and threatened to murder him. The burgesses went on to burn on MARKET Hill as many documents as they could find, while an old woman scattered the ashes to the winds, shouting 'Away with the learning of the clerks, away with it!' Soon after the mayor and burgesses broke into BARNWELL Priory and did what damage they could. 'Town and gown' disturbances continued long after this. (See E. Powell, *The Rising in East Anglia in 1381*, 1893, and Rowland Parker, *Town and Gown. The 700 Years' War in Cambridge*, Patrick Stephens, Cambridge, 1983.)

Such rioting was likely to end with the rioters being imprisoned at the BRIDEWELL in the grounds of Cambridge

Castle. The records for the period 1332–4 show many trials by jury for theft and murder, and a surprisingly large number of acquittals. Yet Iohannes Godeknaue and Iohannes le Whyt, who stole three circlets and chapelets and a piece of green cloth valued at £10, were both sentenced to be hanged. Others pleaded that they were guilty, but were clerks (priests), and were released to await the King's permission for purgation. One man attested that on 12 April 1334 as he stopped in the angle of a wall at Wimpole to relieve himself, a man hit him on the head with a battle-axe, and was hit in return with a cudgel. The accused was returned to prison to await royal pardon, but died there 'of natural causes', as did many others. Conditions in the bridewell were no doubt insanitary. (See Elizabeth G. Kimball, ed., *A Cambridgeshire Gaol Delivery Roll 1332–1334*, Cambridge Antiquarian Record Society, 1978.) Another bridewell, later known as the Spinning House, or HOBSON'S Workhouse stood in St Andrew's Street where the old Police Station of 1901 now is. Founded by Hobson the carrier in 1628, originally as a workhouse, it was later used 'for the confinement of such lewd women as the Proctors apprehended in houses of ill fame', though the Corporation also made use of it, 'and the crier of the town is often there to discipline the ladies of pleasure with his whip'. (Quoted in H. P. Stokes, *Outside the Barnwell Gate*, Cambridge Antiquarian Society Publications, no. 47, 1915.)

The name 'bridewell' comes from the house of correction in London near the St Bride's Well (originally St Bridget's) off Fleet Street. The Cambridge street is named after Royal Bridewell Hospital, part of St Thomas's Hospital, former owner of the land, which was transferred to Savoy Hospital in the 1550s.

The beginning of the University

Simon LANGHAM (d. 1376) Archbishop of Canterbury, Chancellor of England, and Cardinal, was also Bishop of Ely, and thus, as Visitor (a kind of ombudsman) and Patron, had close connection with Peterhouse, several of whose members are commemorated in the same neighbourhood. One of these was John HOLBROOK (d. 1437), Master 1418–31, Chancellor 1428 and 1429–31 and chaplain to Henry V and Henry VI – was he at the battle of Agincourt? This is the oldest college, founded in 1284. CLARE College succeeded in 1326, and was named after Elizabeth, Lady Clare, who refounded it as Clare House in 1338. (Presumably Clare *Road* was named after the college.) In 1347 came PEMBROKE College, originally the Hall of Valence Marie, named after Mary, widow of Aymer de Valence, Earl of Pembroke, who according to legend was killed at a tournament on his wedding day. It was later richly endowed by Henry VI. Edmund GONVILLE (d. 1351) founded Gonville Hall in 1349, completed by William BATEMAN, Bishop of NORWICH, and by Sir Walter Manny. William LYNDE-WODE (*c.* 1375–1446) was educated there, later becoming a Fellow of Pembroke. He wrote a great edition of the legislation of the province of Canterbury, became Bishop of St David's and assisted in the foundation of Eton College and King's. He was heavily involved in the proceedings against the heretical Lollards, who were burned at the stake (see WYCLIFFE): 'even a man of fine learning', writes a recent historian, 'could not shrink from frying his fellow-men'. (See *Ecclesiastical Law Journal*, 2 (1990–92), pp. 268–72, and B. E. Ferme, *Canon Law in Medieval England, a Study of William Lyndwood's 'Provinciale'*, LAS Rome, 1996.)

In the early sixteenth century the hostility between different parts of England was shown when students from the north burned the gate of GONVILLE Hall and sacked the college, which declined for many years until it was revived by John Caius (1510–73), an eminent physician, whose name then joined that of Gonville in the name of the college.

Meanwhile Trinity Hall was founded by the same William BATEMAN, Bishop of NORWICH, in 1350, as a 'perpetual College of Scholars in the Civil and Canon Law'. It still remains known for its lawyers and judges, though all subjects are now taught. Bateman died suddenly and was buried before the altar of the Cathedral of Avignon, where at that time one of the two rival Popes resided.

The Guild of Corpus Christi and the Guild of St Mary jointly founded Corpus Christi College in 1352. William BATEMAN was again involved, in obtaining a new site for the college, whose first Master was Thomas ELTISLEY. It was in Eltisley's time as Master (1352–76) and that of his successor that the beautiful Old Court of Corpus Christi was built.

John WARKWORTH (d. 1500), Master of Peterhouse 1473–1500, is the reputed author of *Warkworth's Chronicle* of the reign of Edward IV. He left this to the college, which has a portrait of him.

These six colleges, all founded in a period of less than seventy years, marked a first step. The Black Death of the mid-fourteenth century, which killed between a quarter and a third of the population of Europe, hindered further progress in what has been called a 'third-rate university', in comparison with Oxford, which had already nurtured several scholars of international repute. However, the foundation of KING'S College in 1440–1 by Henry VI began to influence the rivalry. The college was

Trumpington Street

given unusual independence, so that the first Provost (Master), William MILLINGTON (d. 1466?) felt obliged to resign, because the exemption of King's from the University's jurisdiction conflicted with his oath of fealty to the Chancellor. His successor, John CHEDWORTH (d. 1471), from MERTON College Oxford, seems not to have been tainted by his association with the 'other place'. In fact he may have helped the college to survive, when the Yorkist Edward IV took a dislike to the foundation of Lancastrian Henry VI, by his support of the

Yorkist cause. The vast size of King's College Chapel must have contrasted powerfully with the thatched cottages all round. (See Elisabeth Leedham-Green, *A Concise History of the University of Cambridge*, 1996, which has a large bibliography for both the University and the colleges; also C. G. Griffinhoofe, *Celebrated Cambridge Men A.D. 1390–1908*, Cambridge, 1910.)

The Reformation

Although Luther did not make his stand against the Papacy at Wittenberg till 1517, there had been stirrings much earlier. John WYCLIFFE (d. 1384) was accused of heresy and of holding that the Pope could legitimately be accused by laymen. The translation of the Bible bearing his name preceded Luther's, and he too, like Luther, condemned monasticism. His followers at Oxford, many of them the so-called 'Lollards', displeased Henry VI, and influenced him in choosing orthodox Cambridge for his new and great foundation, KING'S (1440–1). This led at once to the foundation of QUEENS' (1446–8) by Henry's wife, Margaret of Anjou (and later by the Queen of Edward IV, Elizabeth Woodville), 'to laud and honneure of sexe femenine', though women did not join the college for some 500 years. The third Provost of King's, Robert WOODLARK, then founded St Catharine's (1473), and Cambridge began to close in on Oxford in the pursuit of fame. The first monastery to be dissolved (in 1496) was ST RADEGUND'S, whose great benefactor, if not founder, had been King MALCOLM IV of Scotland (not the one who succeeded Macbeth). (KING Street has been thought to relate to him, but was called Walls Lane till *c.* 1798, when the present HOBSON Street was called King Street.)

JESUS College took over its decayed buildings, its founder intending a continuance of the religious traditions of the nunnery.

All these colleges remained true on the whole to medieval traditions. CHRIST'S, founded 1505 by the mother of Henry VII, LADY MARGARET Beaufort, was granted statutes giving new importance to classical studies, and thus to the new spirit of the Renaissance, moving slowly in from Italy. ST JOHN'S, founded 1509 by the same lady (yet still without advantage to her gender), took over the grounds of the Augustinian Hospital of St John (c. 1135). A third college to take over a monastic foundation, that of [BUCKINGHAM] College, was MAGDALENE (1542). This was an offshoot of the great Benedictine Abbey of CROWLAND near Peterborough of which the Dukes of Buckingham were benefactors. Then came Henry VIII's royal foundation of unprecedented size and magnificence, TRINITY (1546), using the wealth of the dissolved monasteries throughout England to create a college that should be the bulwark of the new order of things ushered in by the Reformation. But for the insistence of Catherine Parr, the wife who survived him, Henry might have dissolved the Cambridge colleges along with the purely religious communities. The University had progressed to great prominence in the course of a hundred years.

The grounds of the Dominican monastery remained empty after its dissolution until 1584, when EMMANUEL took them over. The college was intended by its founder, Sir Walter Mildmay, for the training of Protestant clergy, as was SIDNEY SUSSEX, founded in 1594 by the Lady Frances Sidney, Countess of Sussex, occupying the Franciscans' site. The formerly Catholic colleges and new foundations were now wholly reformed. For over 200 years there were no new foundations, until the founding of DOWNING (1800).

Yet the struggle between Catholic and Protestant had continued throughout the sixteenth century, with disastrous consequences for some. One who maintained his freedom throughout his life was [ERASMUS] of Rotterdam (*c.* 1466–1536) who taught at Cambridge in 1511, staying for about three years, off and on. He was probably Lady Margaret Professor of Theology, but also taught Greek, the 'new' key to the Scriptures, which he used in translating the New Testament into Latin. The most famous scholar in Europe in his day, he had just published his *In Praise of Folly*, attacking monasticism and the corruptions of the Church, and in this way paved the way for the Reformation. However, while he did not side with Luther, always preferring peace to violence, his writings were forbidden by the Pope in 1559 and again in 1590. He was at Queens' College, and complained of the Cambridge dons, as well as the beer and the wine, yet preferred to risk the plague in Cambridge rather than drink the beer brewed by his friends at Landbeach. Indeed he spoke later of Cambridge having changed, detesting now 'those chill subtleties which make more for disputation than piety'. He even claimed that by 1518 Cambridge was better at Greek than Oxford. (See H. C. Porter, *Reformation and Reaction in Tudor Cambridge*, 1958.) (Erasmus Close, being off [DARWIN] Drive, and at the other end from FRANCIS DARWIN Court, may refer to Charles Darwin's grandfather Erasmus Darwin (1731–1802) who anticipated some ideas on evolution.)

Others at Cambridge were soon involved in the controversies of Protestant ideas against Catholic ones, inflamed by Henry VIII's divorce from Catherine of ARAGON (1485–1536), his first wife, who had failed to bear him a male heir. Hugh LATIMER (c. 1485–1555), a Fellow of Clare, approved of the divorce but suffered for this as well as for his religious beliefs when Catherine's daughter Mary came to the throne. He was strongly opposed to miraculous images, and popular for his down-to-earth sermons, the most famous being based on the theme of playing cards. Thomas CRANMER (1489–1556), a Fellow of Jesus, suffered similarly at the stake, boldly thrusting his hand into the flames since it had offended by signing both recantations and the recantations of recantations. He had not only consented to the burning of heretics, but had interceded (in vain) for Fisher and Thomas More, Anne Boleyn and Thomas Cromwell. 'He was at once a divine and a courtier', says Macaulay, 'and the combination proved impossible.' Nicholas RIDLEY (c. 1500–55), Fellow and Master of PEMBROKE Hall, was a friend of CRANMER and helped to draw up his great literary achievement, *The Book of Common Prayer*. He too was burned at the stake with LATIMER on 16 October 1555. However, Nicholas METCALFE (1475?–1539), Master of St John's, opposed Henry VIII's divorce and survived, but had to resign the Mastership despite excellent qualifications. He had greatly contributed to the advancement of scholarship and learning in the college, and attracted many benefactions, but Henry's will counted for more.

Cardinal Thomas WOLSEY (c. 1475–1530) had become almost as powerful as the King until he failed to give clear approval to the divorce and was accused of high treason by the faction of Anne Boleyn. He died on the way to London for his trial. He had founded Christ Church, Oxford, well before Henry founded Trinity, and hinted by its sheer size, as well as by placing his own arms above those of the King on the college gatehouse, at the great ambition of clerical advancement he nursed, yet regretted at last having served God less well than he had served the King.

In those fanatical times it was not easy to survive. Ralph [AINSWORTH], who was Master of Peterhouse in 1544, took part in the sale of the Papist processional cross of the University in 1547, and was expelled, on the accession of the Catholic Mary Tudor, as a married man. His successor, Andrew PERNE (*c.* 1519–89) can hardly be blamed by today's standards for his adaptability in surviving the reigns both of Mary and of Elizabeth the Protestant. He did, however, preach when the bodies of the Protestants Fagius and Bucer were exhumed and burned, and then assent when their names were restored to honour by the Senate. Yet he left money to build the library at Peterhouse and to provide most of its contents. Thomas THIRLEBY (*c.* 1506–70) of Trinity Hall, Bishop of Norwich and of Ely, had strong Catholic sympathies, but was favoured by CRANMER. He opposed the *First Prayer Book* of Edward VI and the Act of Uniformity which imposed its use, though he accepted it when passed. As a Catholic he was favoured by Mary, but refused the Oath of Supremacy under Elizabeth and was imprisoned. He was 'not a very severe persecutor of heretics', although a vicar of Babraham, John Hullier, who refused to recant, was tried for heresy in Great St Mary's and burned to death on Jesus Green. Only two other Protestants in Ely diocese suffered the same fate, at Ely.

Matthew PARKER (1504–75) has been associated with Parker Street (Emmanuel Back Lane in the eighteenth century). He too lived in some peril. A moderate, he was in favour under Henry VIII, but was deprived by Mary and lived in obscurity till Elizabeth chose him to be Archbishop of Canterbury. Master of

Corpus Christi, he was very much the scholar, and is remembered there for the magnificent collection of manuscripts collected by him at the Dissolution of the Monasteries.

Robert [BEAUMONT] (d. 1567) fled in the reign of Mary with other Protestants to Zurich, but returned on Mary's death and was admitted Lady Margaret Professor of Divinity in 1559. Having been a Fellow of Peterhouse, he was Master of Trinity in 1561 and later Vice-Chancellor. He was prominent in the movement of Calvinists at Cambridge against conforming to the ordinances of Elizabeth and PARKER, and supported the anti-ritualistic party of the Church. (See, however, Joseph Beaumont, below, p. 47.)

[WEST] Road may be just the counterpart of EAST Road. (It was 'New Road' in the time of the nineteenth-century diarist Josiah Chater.) However, it runs alongside King's Fellows' Garden, and so may call to mind Nicholas West (1461–1533), a Fellow of King's who became Bishop of Ely (after a madcap youth, according to Fuller). Promoted by the favour of WOLSEY, he was chaplain to Catherine of ARAGON, and opposed divorce proceedings against her. He built the splendid Renaissance chapel roof at Ely, with the words in Latin over the entrance, 'By the grace of God I am what I am'. He did not live long enough to experience the conflicts of conscience in the middle of the sixteenth century.

Roger ASCHAM (1515–68) of St John's, however, was tutor to Elizabeth while she was still a princess, and then Latin secretary to Mary, being specially permitted to continue in his Protestantism. In 1558, after Elizabeth came to the throne, he was appointed her private tutor. His *Toxophilus* promotes the cause of archery as a sport and a preparation for war. His most famous work, *The Scholemaster* (1570), deals with the education of boys, advocating gentleness rather than corporal punishment, and is in a clear English prose style. The school named after him began in 1916 as the Cambridge Open Air School for children suffering from tuberculosis, the plague of that time. It moved to Ascham Road in 1928 and closed in 1987. Stephen PERSE (1548–1615) of Caius founded the school named after him which stood in FREE SCHOOL Lane but later moved to Hills Road. (See J. M. Gray, *A History of the Perse School*, 1921, and S. J. D. Mitchell, *Perse. A History of the Perse School 1615–1976*, 1976, and M. A. Scott, *The Perse School for Girls, Cambridge. The First Hundred Years 1881–1981*, 1981.) The almshouses he also founded were transferred to Newnham in 1855–6. (See John A. Gray, ed., *Newnham*, Hanwell Publications, Cambridge, 1977.)

A survivor like Ascham was the financier Sir Thomas GRESHAM (1519–79) of Caius, founder of the Royal Exchange, who was credited, wrongly, with the formulation of 'Gresham's Law', that, in effect, 'bad money drives out good'. Though a Puritan, he lived through the reign of Mary and into that of Elizabeth.

Another Archbishop of Canterbury, Richard BANCROFT (1544–1640), entered Christ's, but was required to leave the college because of its Puritan principles, and went over to Jesus, but was not a Fellow. As Bishop of London he used his pikemen to repel the Earl of Essex's insurrection. In 1608 he was Chancellor of Oxford University. He co-operated in the 'King James' translation of the Bible. Being, it is said, 'arbitrary' and 'irritable' by disposition, though also capable of tact and conciliation, by his strong opposition to Puritans he led many to emigrate to America. Richard [MONTAGUE] (1577–1641), Fellow of King's, Bishop of Chichester and of Norwich, favoured by Charles I with his High Church leanings, was bitterly opposed by the House of Commons, which proposed the burning of a book by him for his alleged leaning towards Catholicism. His leading idea, however, was the catholicity of the English church. He was said to have 'a tartness of writing, very sharp the nib of his pen, and much gall mingled in his ink against such as opposed him'.

From this period date the first maps in the collection by J. Willis Clark and Arthur Gray, *Old Plans of Cambridge 1574–1798*, Part I, Text, and Part II, Maps, 1921.

The Renaissance and science

The trials of the clergy became less severe as Protestantism established itself as the state religion, though Catholics and Puritans still suffered. Cambridge street-names still remember men of the latter part of the sixteenth century who were connected with the revival of classical learning, already promoted by ASCHAM. Thomas SACKVILLE (1536–1608) is remembered as the collaborating author of the first English tragedy in blank verse, *Gorboduc*, or *Ferrex and Porrex*, inspired by the Roman tragedies of Seneca. Fulke GREVILLE (1554–1628) of Jesus, a favourite of Elizabeth, was a poet and dramatist, influenced by Plato. He was a friend and the biographer of Sir Philip SIDNEY, whose cousin founded Sidney SUSSEX. Another friend of Sidney was Arthur GOLDING (1536?–1605?), translator of Ovid's *Metamorphoses*, which Shakespeare certainly knew well. (Golding is said to have been educated at Queens', but there is no evidence of this. The street is in a 'Jesus' cluster.) Christopher MARLOWE (1564–93),

36

whose plays are still performed, wrote *Dr Faustus* and *Edward II*, as well as strikingly beautiful poems. He made no secret of his atheism, which would have cost him his life a century earlier, but was killed in a tavern brawl. Cambridge University Marlowe Dramatic Society honours his connection with Corpus Christi and the University. (See Graham Chainey, *A Literary History of Cambridge*, 1985, for Marlowe's time at Cambridge.)

The new sense of nationhood under Elizabeth was given expression by William CAMDEN (1551–1623). His *Britannia* of 1586 is the first comprehensive topographical survey of England. He also wrote a life of Elizabeth. Camden Court and Camden House date from the late 1830s, when the Cambridge Camden Society was founded for the republication of historical documents.

[NEVILLE] Road may recall the name of Thomas Nevile (*c.* 1548–1615), Master of Trinity from 1592, who created out of a warren of older buildings of earlier foundations the splendid Great Court, full of Renaissance spaciousness. No Magdalene connection has been discovered and there is no strong reason for supposing the road is named after him, but he is remembered in Nevile's Court at Trinity. It was he who exchanged with the mayor in 1612–13 land on both sides of the river near Trinity, now part of the Backs, for various pieces of land, the most important of which became known as Parker's Piece, because the estate had been leased to Edward Parker, cook. Ena Mitchell has shown in *Notes on the History of Parker's Piece, Cambridge* (no date), how successive generations have enclosed 'waste land' in this area for private use.

Nicholas FERRAR (1592–1637) of Clare College established at Little Gidding in 1625 a community that has become world-famous through the title of one of T. S. Eliot's *Four Quartets*.

The Church of the Good Shepherd was originally named after him. The community was broken up by Parliament in 1647, but revived in recent times.

With the seventeenth century a new spirit of inquiry emerged, well represented in the work of Francis Bacon (1561–1626), a Trinity man, whose titles were Baron VERULAM and Viscount ST ALBANS. His rejection of the authority of Aristotle and demand for knowledge based on argued evidence laid a theoretical basis for modern science, which had already begun in the work of William GILBERT (1540–1603), author of the first great scientific book published in England, *De Magnete* (1600), 'one of the chief landmarks in the history of science'. (See R. T. Gunther, *Early Science in Cambridge*, 1937.) In this work Gilbert, a Johnian, assembled everything then known about magnets, and conceived the idea that the earth itself was a giant magnet. He invented two instruments by which seamen could determine latitude without seeing sun, moon or stars. Just as important was the work of William HARVEY (1578–1657) of Caius, who is credited with establishing the circulation of the blood. Another Caius man, Francis GLISSON (1597–1677) lectured on anatomy at Cambridge and produced almost the first English medical monograph, on rickets. 'Glisson's capsule' is the name given to the sheath of the liver.

Isaac BARROW (1630–77), first Lucasian Professor of Mathematics, resigned in favour of Newton, his pupil, in 1669, in order to devote himself to theology. In 1672, as Master of Trinity, he founded the library. Charles II who appointed him said he had chosen the best scholar in England for the post, but thought less well of his sermons, which sometimes lasted for over three hours. The Dean of Westminster was so wearied of these, so the story goes, that he had the organ played to drown them, but their language has been highly praised. Barrow's statue is in Trinity Chapel.

Isaac NEWTON (1642–1727), while absent from Cambridge during the plague (1665–6), invented the binomial theorem and differential calculus, computed the area of the hyperbola, and conceived the idea of universal gravitation; he later founded the emission theory of light. ([DIAMOND] Close is in the area where Trinity names predominate, including Newton's. Might this be an allusion to the dog of this name, which knocked over a lighted candle, and so destroyed many of Newton's papers? Humphrey Newton, who was Newton's sizar, or servant, in the 1680s, states categorically that his master kept no dog, but the story may still have been the inspiration of the street-name.) One of many delightful stories about Newton's absent-mindedness relates how he ignored a guest he had invited for dinner, how the guest ate the one dinner Newton had sent for, and how Newton at last became aware of the empty plate. 'But for the evidence of my own senses', Newton exclaimed, 'I could have sworn I had not dined tonight.' His modesty is remembered in his saying he had been like a boy picking up a pebble or a prettier shell than ordinary, 'whilst the great ocean of truth lay all undiscovered before me'. Yet his ambition was to penetrate the secret of the alchemical Philosophers' Stone, and to interpret the Old Testament in a mystical sense: 'he regarded the universe', said Geoffrey Keynes, 'as a cryptogram set by the Almighty', which he would solve. An apple tree outside Trinity Great Gate in front of Newton's study, and another in the Botanic Garden are of the same kind, 'Flower of Kent', as the one at Woolsthorpe near Grantham, where, Newton said, he hit on his theory of gravity after watching an apple fall.

Well known to Newton was Samuel PEPYS (1633–1703),

who came to MAGDALENE in 1651 and often returned, partly because of litigation over family property in Impington – a John Pepys built Impington Hall – partly to renew college acquaintance: 'and there drank my bellyfull of their beer, which pleased me as the best I ever drank'. He was tempted to accept an invitation to be presented as Provost to King's – *that* would have been a startling role for him – but decided against. Magdalene profited by his bequest of exactly 3,000 books, and the manuscript of his famous diary. (See Chainey, *A Literary History of Cambridge*, p. 37, above, for Pepys and Cambridge.) [BRAMPTON] in Cambridgeshire was Pepys's family estate, though this may well not be why the street is so named.

John FLAMSTEED (1646–1719) met Newton in 1674, and gave him great help in writing his 'Principia', for which Newton was ungrateful. The first astronomer-royal of England, he laid the basis for modern astronomy, and undertook a complete catalogue of all the stars, which was a great benefit to navigators, and part of which Newton plagiarised.

A practical man was Thomas HOBSON (1544?–1631), the carrier, who was part of a consortium that provided clean water in 'Hobson's Conduit'. The course of one part of this is marked on the pavement opposite the main Post Office. Hobson would not allow his horses to be hired out of turn, hence 'Hobson's Choice' – the one he decided on. (See W. D. Bushell, *Hobson's Conduit*, 1938.) He owned much land in Chesterton, where the Hall was probably built by him or his family, but is buried in St Bene't's Church.

IZAAK WALTON's (1593–1683) *The Compleat Angler* was first published in 1653. ANGLER'S Way speaks for itself. Both are near the river, as is GRAYLING Close, named by the builder Peter Ginn after the fish. WATER Lane and Street, recorded with this name by 1580, are named after the landowner Alexander Attewater, recorded in 1279.

Sir Francis PEMBERTON (1625–97) is perhaps the best known of the Pemberton family of Trumpington. He was Lord Chief Justice of the King's Bench, which did not save him from imprisonment. (Pepys also suffered this fate as did many of the High Stewards of the Borough.) Christopher Pemberton, whose office was in Grove Lodge, Trumpington Street, from 1798 till his death in 1850, aged eighty-five, preceded the solicitor's business of Clement [FRANCIS] (1818–80), which became the practice most closely involved with the University and colleges. (See Christopher Jackson, *A Cambridge Bicentenary. The History of a Legal Practice 1789–1989*, Morrow and Co., Bungay, 1990.) [FRANCIS] Passage is near Norwich and Bateman Streets, both associated with Trinity Hall, of which Clement Francis was a member. (Though small, this passage may still have been meant to honour him. Nelson fared no better.) The Trumpington Estate is entailed to carry the name of Pemberton. Sir Francis Pemberton, the present owner, is the son of William Warburton WINGATE, a Cambridge doctor; he married Viola Pemberton and perpetuated the name of Wingate in naming the street.

The GUNNING family is also closely associated with Cambridge. Peter Gunning (1614–84), Bishop of Ely, a member of several colleges, is said to have written the prayer 'for all sorts and conditions of men'. His tomb is in Ely Cathedral. Other Gunnings were Fellows of St John's, as was Henry Gunning (1768–1854), author of the *Reminiscences of the University, Town and County of Cambridge from the year 1780*. Francis John Gunning was a partner with Clement Francis (see above) from 1838.

When a judge like Pemberton could be imprisoned, it is not surprising that Thomas TENISON risked the same fate when he supported the seven bishops who in 1688 rejected James II's attempt at removing disabilities of Catholics. A Fellow of Corpus Christi, and vicar of Great St Andrew's, he became Archbishop of Canterbury, and took part in founding the Society for the Propagation of the Gospel. He preached a funeral sermon for Nell Gwynne, whom he had found penitent, reproved William III to his face for his adultery, and was praised for his ministrations during the plague. His friend Evelyn praised him as a preacher. Swift, like James II, thought him a dull man, 'who had a horror of anything like levity in his clergy, especially of whist' – but Swift had been denied preferment by him. Equally stern was Jeremy COLLIER (1650–1726) of Caius, author of a *Short View of the Immorality and Profaneness of the English Stage*, in which he denounced Dryden and Congreve. His independence showed itself when he sided with the bishops who refused to swear allegiance to William III and Mary II. He even absolved on the scaffold two of those who plotted to assassinate William in 1696.

Alderman Edward STOREY (d. 1693), a bookseller, was the founder of Storey's Charity: his house was no. 15 Magdalene Street. Almshouses bearing his name were built before 1688, in 1729, and 1844 on the south side of NORTHAMPTON Street, behind the street, and at the north-west end of the site bounded by MOUNT PLEASANT, ALBION Row and SHELLY Row. 'Michel's' restaurant in Northampton Street occupies one of these houses. (See Joan Fitch, 'The foundation of Edward Storey', *Cambridgeshire Local History Council Bulletin*, 35 (1980), pp. 6–10, and H. M. Larke and S. Shield, *The Foundation of Edward Storey. A Short History 1693–1980*, 1980.)

Orchard Street

GREEN Street is said to have been so named because it was shut off during a plague, after which grass had grown to an extraordinary height. In fact it was part of the estate of Oliver Green MD (1563–1623), of Caius, a native of Trumpington. (See Arthur B. Gray, *Cambridge Revisited*, 1921, 'Green Street: Today and Yesterday', pp. 95–106.)

The Civil War

The century saw not only the questioning of Aristotle's authority but of that of the King. Oliver CROMWELL (1599–1658) matriculated at SIDNEY SUSSEX (where his head is still preserved) and sat for Cambridge in the Parliaments of 1640. In that year he was made a Freeman of Cambridge. In 1642 he seized the magazine in Cambridge Castle, and hindered the carrying of the University plate to the King. In 1644 about two hundred Fellows, half the total, had been ejected. Cromwell fortified the town, making it his headquarters; the remains of the bastions he had made still overlook MAGRATH Avenue, and in the Second World War it was even planned to place field guns there. His house at Ely is preserved as a museum, as is the school he attended in Huntingdon. (See Clive Holmes, *The Eastern Association in the English Civil War*, 1974.)

Thomas FAIRFAX (1612–71) matriculated at St John's and became the brilliant commander-in-chief of the Parliamentary army. He behaved with reckless courage at the battle of Naseby, where he captured a royalist standard with his own hands. MILTON looked to him, in the sonnet beginning 'Fairfax, whose name in arms through Europe rings . . .', to restore peace. Despite his allegiance to Parliament he was against the seizure of Charles I, and tried to prevent his execution. In 1660 he headed the commission sent to negotiate with Charles II for his return to England.

In 1644 Fairfax took prisoner the Duke of ALBEMARLE, George Monck (1608–70), commander of the royalist Scots in Ireland, who later conquered Scotland for Parliament, and yet helped to restore Charles II and rose to high favour, defeating the Dutch at sea. He was Chancellor of the University in 1682.

As in the sixteenth century, it was possible, though risky, to change sides without incurring retribution.

SHIRLEY Grove and School are named after James Shirley (1596–1666), author of some forty plays, a graduate of St Catharine's (who were allocated land in this area in the Chesterton Inclosures of 1840). The college dramatic society bears his name. He followed the Earl of Newcastle in the Civil Wars. His death was a result of terror and exposure on the occasion of the Great Fire of London.

John MILTON (1608–74) was an undergraduate at Christ's, where a mulberry traditionally said to have been planted by him still gives plenty of fruit. (Milton Road leads to the village of Milton; only Milton's Walk, alongside Christ's, is named after the poet.) His first great poem, 'On the Morning of Christ's Nativity', was written in 1629. In the same year, or in 1631, the year in which he became BA, he wrote of King's College Chapel, so it has been thought, in his 'Il Penseroso':

> But let my due feet never fail,
> To walk the studious cloister's pale,
> And love the high embowed roof,
> With antique pillars' massy proof,
> And storied windows richly dight,
> Casting a dim religious light.
> There let the pealing organ blow,
> To the full-voiced choir below,
> In service high, and anthems clear,
> As may with sweetness, through mine ear,
> Dissolve me into ecstasies,
> And bring all heaven before mine eyes.

Also while at Christ's he wrote 'L'Allegro', the poem on Shakespeare, and two epitaphs on HOBSON. His friend

Edward King, the subject of his *Lycidas*, was at Christ's with him. (See Chainey, *A Literary History of Cambridge*, p. 37 above, for Milton's time at Cambridge.) In the Civil War he was appointed Latin secretary to the Council of State, dealing with diplomacy and defending the execution of Charles I in a work addressed to the rest of Europe. At the Restoration he was arrested and fined, but released. He then set about completing *Paradise Lost*, the work for which he is best known, seeking to 'justify the ways of God to man'.

The Marquis of MONTROSE (1612–50) invaded England in 1640 with the Scottish Covenanters. After a defeat he escaped abroad, but invaded Scotland in 1650, was again defeated and hanged in Edinburgh the same year.

[FRANK's] Lane is probably named, not after Mark Frank (1613–64), Master of Pembroke, but some unknown man whose first name was Frank. The name existed before any buildings were there.

Sir Richard FANSHAWE (1608–66), a zealous royalist and a fellow-commoner at Jesus, was in attendance on Prince Charles during the Civil War. He was MP for Cambridge University and wrote poems, as well as translating Horace, Guarini and Camoês. In his many sufferings in the royal cause he was often sustained by his wife's courage.

Another unwavering royalist was Tobias RUSTAT (1606?–94). He was servant to Charles II as Prince of Wales, and a benefactor, though not a member of Jesus College. (Rustat happens to be an anagram of Stuart). In 1667 he left £1,000 to the University Library for the purchase of books. There had been no such fund till then. A Rustat scholarship was awarded to S. T. COLERIDGE.

Joseph [BEAUMONT] (1616–69), Master of Peterhouse was

a royalist, ejected like many others in 1644. His poem *Psyche*, some 30,000 lines long, is about the journey of the soul through life to eternal felicity. After the Restoration he was appointed Master of Jesus, later returning to his old college Peterhouse as Master. (See, however, Robert Beaumont, above, p. 34.)

The controversy over religion continued in 1686, when Judge Jeffreys (of the 'Bloody Assizes') was given authority to revise college statutes, presumably in order to remove bars against Catholics, who were favoured by James II. This led to Joshua [BASSET], who had quickly declared himself a Catholic, becoming Master of Sidney Sussex, and to the temporary revision of the college's statutes to allow Catholics to be admitted. (There may well have been someone else who was intended in the street-name.)

The eighteenth century

In this century science and classical learning were both popular with scholars. FLAMSTEED'S astronomical work was continued by Sir William HERSCHEL (1738–1822) who as a boy played in a German band before coming to England. Here, in an astonishing climb to fame, he observed the stars and in 1781 discovered the planet Uranus. In 1789 he discovered a sixth satellite of Saturn, and later more than 2,000 nebulae. His son Sir John (1792–1871) went to Cape Town to study the southern skies, and among many other great achievements made a catalogue of double stars. Sir John was one of the most famous scientists of his day, and is buried in Westminster Abbey near the grave of Newton, where Sir William his father and Sir William his son (d. 1917), author of the fingerprint system, are also commemorated. In the road next to Herschel Road John ADAMS (1819–92), another astronomer, is remembered. (All three astronomers are on land belonging to St John's.) Adams, having noticed as an undergraduate 'irregularities' in the motion of Uranus, discovered they were caused by yet another new planet, Neptune, only to find the planet had been discovered the same year by Leverrier. He was celebrated internationally, and researched later into the theory of the moon's motion.

Henry CAVENDISH (1731–1810) of Trinity, after whom the Cavendish Laboratory is named, in 1798 weighed the earth, but he cared more for investigation than for publication, and few knew what he had done. He anticipated Faraday and Ohm in electrical studies, and constructed a model torpedo fish which could deliver shocks even in salt water. His great discovery, completed by RAYLEIGH, also of Trinity, was of the inert gas argon, and he was the first to understand hydrogen. His many other discoveries also remained unknown for many years. He was so shy he 'held no communication with his female domestics', and would utter a shrill cry at parties, as he shuffled quickly from room to room, seeming to be annoyed if looked at. A contemporary said he probably uttered fewer words in the course of his life than any man who had ever lived to be eighty.

The so-called Augustan Age of the early eighteenth century, named after the Emperor Augustus, was proud to imitate the Roman Empire. The SENATE HOUSE, designed by James Gibbs in 1722 on so-called Senate House Hill, is a sign of this, suggesting by its name a Roman senate. It is, so to speak, the parliament of the University. Degrees are also conferred here. Latin and Greek were prized not only for themselves, but as hints for gentlemen on how to relive the ideals of Roman landowners, and Richard BENTLEY (1662–1742) was one who benefited by this. He was regarded as the foremost classical scholar in England, but as Master of Trinity indulged his self-assertiveness to the uttermost. He dominated the Fellows, but escaped miraculously the law-suits they brought against him for spending the college's money recklessly, especially on expensive improvements to his own Lodge. He was a rude, witty, avaricious, autocratic tyrant, who did, however, build an observatory for Newton's followers over the Great Gate, as well as a chemical laboratory. He was praised by his grandson for his good-natured willingness to show the boy his books – though these all turned out to have pictures of cadavers with anatomical illustrations. He was satirised by Alexander Pope in *The Dunciad*. (See the chapter on him in G. M. Trevelyan's *Trinity College, an Historical Sketch*, 1946.)

A rebel of this time was Christopher ANSTEY, Fellow of King's in 1748–54, who was refused his MA by the University for having ridiculed the authorities in the declaration he was required, and probably as a member of King's declined, to make (see MILLINGTON, p. 28). He was the author of the highly fashionable *The New Bath Guide* (1766), a social satire in verse, still popular in Bath, describing the adventures of the Blunderhead family, and written at Anstey Hall, Trumpington. A keen huntsman, he chased into Emmanuel College a fox which ran round the pond and escaped over a wall.

A humbler man was Richard PORSON (1759–1808), Regius Professor of Greek, though he spent most of his time in London. He lost his Fellowship at Trinity for refusing to take holy orders, but devoted himself to scholarship. 'I am quite satisfied', he said, with a degree of modesty, 'if, three hundred years hence, it shall be said that "one Porson lived towards the end of the eighteenth century, who did a great deal for the text of Euripides".' He is credited with the witticism that the prospect of a Fellow of Trinity was 'a long vista with a church [at Coton] at the end of it'. (Fellows who wished to marry were in his day obliged to resign and take up a parish living.) It was said of him late in life that he would rather drink ink than not drink at all; he confessed himself to having drunk a bottle of embrocation. 'I never can recollect him', said Byron, 'except as drunk or brutal, and generally both.'

A gentleman brought up on classical learning was the statesman and diplomatist Lord CHESTERFIELD (1694–1773) of Trinity Hall, remembered now for his *Letters* to his natural son, advising him how to live. There is an essay on these by Virginia Woolf, who admired him, though Dr Johnson said the letters 'teach the morals of a whore, and the manners of a dancing-master'.

William WARREN (1683–1745), whose name appears in the same Trinity Hall cluster, was a Fellow of that college in 1712, and Minister of St Edward's Church in 1716. 'Warren's Book' is a collection of manuscripts and documents relating to the history of Trinity Hall.

Horace WALPOLE (1717–97), himself a great and delightful writer of letters, devoured Chesterfield's on their publication in 1774. His 'Gothick' house at Strawberry Hill can still be visited, and his *The Castle of Otranto* is still read. He was a son of Sir Robert WALPOLE (1676–1745), Prime Minister, as much praised as vilified, like many another politician, who laid the foundations of free trade and British Colonial policy, but is more often remembered for his opposition to the government's encouragement of investment in the 'South Sea Bubble', while making money from it himself. Both father and son were Kingsmen. However, the name of the road was suggested, in 1939, by Trinity Hall.

Two poets of this time are remembered. Thomas GRAY (1716–71) accompanied Horace WALPOLE on a 'grand tour' of the Continent, and like him wrote excellent letters. His best-known poem is his 'Elegy in a Country Churchyard', full of quotations used today. His 'Ode to Music' (1769), written for the installation as Chancellor of the Duke of GRAFTON, who had secured for him the Professorship of History, speaks of 'willowy Camus' lingering with delight at the beauty of the Cambridge scene. He was at Peterhouse, but left it for Pembroke, after a trick played on him by undergraduates. William COWPER (1731–1800) who visited Cambridge but never lived or studied here, is remembered for several hymns, including 'Hark my Soul! It is the Lord', and 'God moves in a mysterious way', as well as for 'John Gilpin'. He suffered from depressions, after being bullied at school, and tried to take his own life, imagining that God wanted him to re-enact the sacrifice of Isaac by Abraham, with himself as victim. His gentle letters are memorable.

Laurence STERNE'S (1713–68) *Tristram Shandy* was denounced by Horace WALPOLE and many others. It could hardly have been further from classical reason and restraint, and takes many chapters before even coming to the night when Tristram was conceived, after which comes the preface. Tristram disappears from his autobiography altogether after a while. Yet the novel is still enjoyed among other things for its portrayal of 'Uncle Toby', whose hobby is fighting old battles with model forts. It has been influential, especially in Germany. Sterne's *Sentimental Journey* is perhaps the most popular of his works. He graduated from Jesus College.

Sterne is in some ways a precursor of Romanticism, in which William WORDSWORTH (1770–1850) is a very different figure. His love of Nature and his declaration that there cannot be 'any *essential* difference between the language of prose and metrical composition' and that poetry is 'as far as is possible, a selection of the language really spoken by men' broke away from earlier ideas of poetic diction. His *Lyrical Ballads* adhere to these ideas. His *The Prelude* describes his arrival at St John's and his time there. From his room he could look down into Trinity College, and see

> The antechapel where the statue stood
> Of Newton with his prism and silent face,
> The marble index of a mind for ever
> Voyaging through strange seas of Thought, alone.

The statue is still there. Wordsworth also wrote three sonnets on King's College Chapel. His poem beginning 'Aid, glorious Martyrs' is about LATIMER and his fellow Reformers at Cambridge.

A close friend of Wordsworth's was Samuel Taylor COLERIDGE (1772–1834), author of two of the best poems in English, his 'The Ancient Mariner' and 'Kubla Khan'. An undergraduate at Jesus, he broke off for a while to become a dragoon, under the name Silas Tomkyn Comberbacke. Like Wordsworth he was enthusiastic for the French Revolution, but also retracted later after the Reign of Terror. His *Biographia Literaria* did much to introduce German philosophy to English readers. He was also a valuable literary critic. (There are chapters in Chainey, *A Literary History of Cambridge*, p. 37 above, on both Wordsworth and Coleridge and their time at the University.)

Christopher WORDSWORTH (1774–1846), brother of the poet, was Master of Trinity, 1820–41.

The middle of the eighteenth century saw a theological dispute between Benjamin HOADLY (1676–1761) and Thomas SHERLOCK (1678–1761) (whose names appear in parallel streets). Hoadly maintained views almost like those of a modern theologian, having little regard for orthodoxy, and holding that Christians were only required to obey rulers who governed for the good of their people; he also ridiculed church authority, arguing that sincerity was all. He later held that no special benefits were attached to the celebration of the Last Supper, which was a mere commemorative rite. His portrait, in flowing episcopal robes with wide lawn sleeves, by Hogarth, who shared his liberal and humanitarian ideals, is in the Tate Gallery. He was opposed by Sherlock, also a Bishop and also of St Catharine's (and friend at Eton of WALPOLE, the Prime Minister) in the so-called Bangor Controversy. These two may be thought of as symbolically joined, if not reconciled, by the street named after John EACHARD, Master of St Catharine's, 1675–97, which connects them. The founder of St Catharine's was Robert WOODLARK (Wodelarke) (d. 1497), Provost of King's, 1452–79, in the same cluster.

Matthias MAWSON (1683–1770), Bishop of Ely, and Master of Corpus Christi (1724–44) and one of its most generous benefactors, founded twelve scholarships and exhibitions there. His monument is in Ely Cathedral.

Richard GOUGH (1735–1809), fellow-commoner of Corpus Christi, was Director of the Society of Antiquaries, and edited and augmented CAMDEN's *Britannia*, for which he made excursions all over England for twenty years. He translated *The Arabian Nights* but has been called a 'rigid presbyterian'. William STUKELEY (1687–1765), also of Corpus Christi, shared in the founding of that Society, and wrote a study of

Stonehenge and Druidism, which was for him 'the aboriginal patriarchal religion'. His friends called him 'the arch-druid of his age'. He cured his gout partly by using an 'oleum arthriticum', partly by going for long rides in search of antiquities. He was a particular friend of Isaac NEWTON. Baron GWYDIR came into the possession of the BARN-WELL Abbey estate in 1809, after which the remains of the monastery were rapidly destroyed for the sake of the stone. His family estates in County Caernarvon included Gwydir Forest, near Ruthin. His wife was a descendant of the PANTON family. Thomas Panton was Equerry to George II and master of the king's 'running-horses'. In about 1769 he bought all the land round Fen Ditton. This was later bought by Dr HAVILAND (1785–1851), Professor of Anatomy. It has been thought that [PETER'S FIELD] was named after Lord Gwydir, whose name was Peter Burrell.

Benjamin [FLOWER] has as much right as Bernard Flower, glazier (d. 1525) who glazed four windows in King's College Chapel, to be remembered in Flower Street, which was not yet built in 1830, and may have been meant for neither. Benjamin was editor of the *Cambridge Intelligencer* (1793–1803). He commented unfavourably when a cadaver used for anatomy by Dr Richard Watson, Bishop of Llandaff (after whom Llandaff Chambers in Regent Street are named), was tipped into the Cam. For this he was summoned before the House of Lords for alleged libel on the Bishop, sentenced to six months' imprisonment in Newgate, and fined £100. The *Intelligencer* was opposed to the war with France at the time of the French Revolution, to the slave trade and to the corrupt representative of the county in Parliament (see RUTLAND, p. 101). It advocated liberty of speech and of the press. Flower also printed *The Fall of*

Robespierre, of which COLERIDGE wrote the first act. Because of this Coleridge was accused of Jacobinism. BLOSSOM Street, nearby, may have been named by association. (The slum, as it was, is described in C. Russell, 'Gas Lane and Blossom Street', BPhil thesis, 'Exeter', 1976.)

A less well-known man of this period was Richard WHEELER of PETTY CURY, who in the late eighteenth and early nineteenth centuries was a basket-maker: there were plenty of willows for this purpose. He owned land in the parish of St Clement's. Yet another, who served the University well, was John [NICHOLSON] (1730–96), the bookseller, and proprietor of a circulating library, known as 'Maps', who lugged his volumes to one college after another. His full-length portrait, looking benign, hangs in the University Library. However, there is no apparent connection with the street bearing his name, nor is there one connecting it with the bookseller Sygar Nicholson, whose stock of heretical books was burned in 1529 or 1530. At all events, no one else in the DNB has a better claim to be remembered.

War against Napoleon

While MORTLOCK was swindling the public, James BURLEIGH, a prominent landowner and carrier, who profited by Mortlock's sale of council land, made available sixty horses and eight wagons to help resist invasion. There is a portrait of him wearing a round hat with a bearskin, a black cockade and black feather, with the uniform of the Patriotic Association of Cambridge Volunteers. JAMES Street is named after him, and [NORFOLK] Street, almost a continuation of Burleigh Street (but not built in 1830, when the nearest to it was a lane leading to a workhouse), was presumably named after his father-in-law, William Norfolk, who was butler to the Master of Jesus, 1720–65, Mayor in 1769, Paymaster and Treasurer of the Cambridgeshire Militia. The father-in-law's family lived in Little Trinity, Jesus Lane, 1708–95.

The third Duke of GRAFTON (1735–1811), Chancellor of the University, descendant of Charles II, and owner from 1810 of the land round Burleigh Street, had been First Minister after Pitt. His family name, FITZROY, was inherited by Robert Fitzroy (1805–65), who invited DARWIN to accompany him on his voyage in *The Beagle*, which had such revolutionary results in science. Fitzroy instituted the first weather forecasts. (The connection with Grafton and the ownership of the land indicates that it was the Duke who was celebrated here, rather than John Grafton who lit Cambridge by inflammable air or gas obtained from coal, between 1823 and 1830. (See Payne, *Down Your Street*, vol. II, p. 120.) FITZROY Street was earlier named after Blücher, the Prussian general, old 'Forwards!' as he was nicknamed from his favourite word of command, whose arrival at Waterloo sealed the victory over Napoleon of the Duke of WELLINGTON (1769–1852). When the Duke arrived in Cambridge in 1835, he was received with rapturous enthusiasm. 'He was escorted into town by about a thousand horsemen', and the crowd unharnessed the horses from his carriage to drag him to the Senate House themselves. Earlier, Blücher had been treated by the crowd in the same way. Sir Charles James NAPIER (1782–1853) fought against Napoleon's generals in Spain. (Napier Street was so named in 1912; it had till then been ALBERT Street). Admiral Sir Charles Napier (1786–1860) fought against Napoleon at sea. The victory over Napoleon's

---

fleet by Lord NELSON (1758–1805) at TRAFALGAR in 1805 is remembered in two very small streets, Nelson himself in an even smaller one.

George IV and his wife

As Prince REGENT, GEORGE IV (1762–1830) visited BARNWELL, though not Cambridge itself. He married CAROLINE of BRUNSWICK in 1795, but quickly left her for Mrs Fitzherbert, whom he had secretly married in 1785. He accused the Princess of adultery, though he was not guiltless himself, and on succeeding to the throne in 1820 tried to prevent her return, excluding her at his [CORONATION] from Westminster Abbey, where she beat on the door to be admitted. The King's relative unpopularity is evidenced by the number of streets in Cambridge named after her. In 1830 George Street was, however, the name of NEWMARKET Road from East Road onwards out of town.

Queen Victoria's reign

A cluster of names off Parker's Piece seems to bring together several men who were active in the early years of VICTORIA'S reign. (Victoria Street is among the cluster. Others named after the Queen came later, as did QUEEN'S Road, named after she visited Cambridge in 1842 and 1847. QUEENS' Lane, however, is named after the College, as is Queens' Green.) Lord [MELBOURNE] (1779–1848) had been at Trinity before becoming Prime Minister in 1835, and was adviser to the young Queen when she came to the throne in 1837. 'I have no doubt [he] is passionately fond of [the Queen] as he might be of his daughter if he had one', wrote Charles Greville, 'and the more because he is a man with a capacity for loving without anything to love. It became his province to educate, instruct and form the most interesting mind and character in the world.' The relationship fascinated the prurient mob: 'Mrs Melbourne', they shouted at the Queen. CLARENDON Street, which comes between Melbourne Place and Victoria Street, relates to the fourth Earl of that name (1800–70), also at Trinity, who later became Lord Privy Seal in 1839, in Melbourne's government. His coat-of-arms with the motto 'Fidei coticula crux' – the Cross is the touchstone of Faith – is on the signboard of the public house in Clarendon Street, and EARL Street clearly relates to him. [PORTLAND] Place, in the same area, has the name of the BENTINCK family, who have a street named after them off CORONATION Street. Lord George Bentinck (1802–48) might have been intended in Portland Place. The other Bentinck, whose name is that of the street parallel to George IV Street, could well be the third Duke of Portland (1738–1809), William Henry Cavendish, Prime Minister in 1783 and in 1807–9, who very much assisted the passing of the Act of [UNION] with Ireland in 1801. (Could Union Road be part of a cluster including him, George IV and the Coronation and thus be named in memory of that important event? There does not appear to have been any Union Workhouse in this area. See Union Lane.)

Prince ALBERT, Victoria's husband, has a small street named after him, off VICTORIA Road. When the Prince came with the Queen from Windsor in 1843, they were met by the Earl of [HARDWICKE], Lord Lieutenant of Cambridgeshire, and a large body of Yeomanry on horseback. Near Grove Lodge in TRUMPINGTON Street

> a lofty triumphal arch decorated with flowers, evergreens and flags had been erected, and within the arch the Mayor and Council in their formalities waited the Queen's approach. Her Majesty escorted by the Whittlesey Yeomanry Cavalry, arrived here at ten minutes to two when the Mayor presented the Mace, which Her Majesty graciously returned and the Council preceded Her Majesty to Trinity College, the Mayor walking by the right of Her Majesty's carriage. Countless crowds were assembled to greet their Sovereign and her Prince, who were received with the most rapturous enthusiasm.

The Prince did a great deal to reform the University, especially in improving the almost non-existent teaching of science.

[LANSDOWNE] is the name of several marquises. The road off Madingley Road where the name appears is far from the cluster of Melbourne, Clarendon, etc., but could relate to the third Marquis (1780–1863), a 'very moderate Whig', who held office under Melbourne. He too was a Trinity man (the street is on what was once Trinity land) and was active in the abolition of the slave trade. Another possible candidate is the Marquis of Lansdowne, who replaced Pitt, on his death in 1806, as one of the MPs for the University, and was later Chancellor of the Exchequer.

There were two Earls of [DERBY] who were politicians in the nineteenth century. The fourteenth Earl (1799–1869) was Prime Minister three times, but graduated in Oxford, whereas his son, the fifteenth Earl (1826–93) of Trinity, Cambridge, was Indian secretary in his father's ministry, a member of the Cambridge University Commission, Foreign Secretary under his father and Disraeli, and closely connected with three other universities. If either was intended – and in their day both were household names – the fifteenth Earl is the more likely. The Earl of Derby pub near the railway station must refer also to one of them. [STANLEY] is the family name of the Derbys, but Stanley Road could conceivably refer to Henry Morton Stanley, the explorer (1841–1904), who lectured on 'The Dark Continent' at the Guildhall in 1878, and achieved great fame. Prime Minister in 1852, 1858–9 and 1866–8 with Derby, Benjamin Disraeli, Earl of BEACONSFIELD (1804–81) (cf. Beaconsfield Terrace in Sturton Town), was Prime Minister alone in 1874–80. His new Conservatism aimed at social reform and the conciliation of the working classes. In foreign policy he led a dramatic assertion of British national interests. His great opponent Gladstone said, when the Liberals won in 1880, 'the downfall of Beaconsfieldism is like the vanishing of some vast magnificent castle in an Italian romance'. He said of Gladstone, 'He has not a single redeem-ing defect.'

There were also two Earls of Rosebery, whose family name was [PRIMROSE], and again the one who was Prime Minister (and Foreign Secretary) was educated at Oxford, whereas the other was at Pembroke, Cambridge. The former, Archibald Philip, fifth Earl (1847–1929) was a Gladstonian liberal who opposed the idea of the Empire as a means of aggrandisement. The second, grandfather of the first, Archibald John, fourth Earl (1783–1868), educated at Pembroke, was an honorary Doctor of Civil Law at Cambridge, a Privy Councillor and a supporter of the Reform Bill of 1832. His Cambridge connec-tions make him the more likely to have been intended. Primrose Street had been begun by 1872, just after his death.

William Ewart GLADSTONE (1809–98) was four times Prime Minister, and likely to have been commemorated for that reason alone. His only memorable connection with Cambridge is through his daughter Helen, who was at Newnham College when in 1881 the question of admitting women to Tripos examinations as of right was being voted upon. She persuaded him to have a special train put on, so that MPs could come to Cambridge and record their vote. The 'Grace', or 'motion', was passed by 398 to 32. Gladstone also planted a tree, in the college grounds, which was dug up by Tory undergraduates, though a tree said to have been planted or provided by him exists near the same spot.

The railway arrived in Cambridge in 1845. In that year the fare from London by the quick train, taking 1 hour 50 minutes, was 10s.6d. first class, 7s.6d. second class. Only one train a day was available for third class; it took four hours and cost 4s.10d. By 1923, when the GREAT EASTERN and Great Northern lines merged, forming the London and North-Eastern Railway, the time taken was 1 hour 5 minutes (See Reginald B. Fellows, *London to Cambridge by Train 1845–1938*, The Oleander Press, 1976.) The last stage coach left Cambridge for London in 1849. The Great Eastern Railway grew out of the Eastern Counties Railway, which had built Cambridge STATION, designed by Francis Thompson or by him and Sancton Wood in time for the opening of the line, although the station of today was not laid out till 1863. The present length of the platform – 1,650 feet – was not reached till just before 1939. (See Alan Warren and Ralph Phillips, *Cambridge Station. A Tribute*, 1987).

With the railway came an extraordinary increase in population, which was 252 in the area of MILL Road in 1801, 6,651 in 1831, 11,848 in 1861 and 25,091 in 1891. Gonville and Caius and

Corpus Christi developed the east and west side of MILL Road (COLLIER, MACKENZIE, GUEST, PEROWNE, MAWSON, TENISON, etc.). Most of the area between Parker's Piece and the railway was built on between 1850 and 1870.

The union referred to in UNION Lane (not Road), called Mill Lane from 1325 to the 1840s, is the workhouse, and thus a reminder of the way the poor were treated in Victorian times. Although the railway brought employment, and the area off East Road saw a housing boom, there was still not enough work for all, and several workhouses existed. One reason was that the poor were driven off the land by eighteenth- and early nineteenth-century Inclosures. After Napoleon, continuing hardships and the introduction of farm machinery led to the burning of haystacks and barns in East Anglia by 'Captain Swing'.

From 1834, the date of the Poor Law, a 'union' was formed of parishes to administer the law, hence the name for a workhouse. Here the poor, not only the able-bodied, but the aged, orphaned and insane, were housed, and required to work if at all capable, like Oliver Twist. 'By the late eighteenth century', writes Michael J. Murphy in *Poverty in Cambridgeshire*, 1978, p. 2, 'HOBSON'S workhouse had become a BRIDEWELL (or prison) possessing cells with iron gratings on the doors and windows . . . In the parishes of St Edward and St Giles it was necessary to add special barred rooms to house the violent and insane.' The construction of the UNION Lane building (1836–87) reflects this. It had originally four wings radiating from a centre, as in a 'panopticon', where a watch could be kept simultaneously in several directions. The gaol on Castle Hill had the same plan.

The workhouse at DITCHBURN Place, off MILL Road, opened in 1838, was later a military hospital, then a maternity hospital, and is now a model 'sheltered housing' scheme, named after Douglas and Doris Ditchburn, Master and Matron, 1934–56. The memories of childhood by a man who stayed there in 1907–10, when it was still a workhouse, include playing in the backyard with two old tramps and 'other down-and-outs' before being rescued by the Matron, who dressed him in clean under-clothes and 'a navy sailor suit with a lovely blue and white collar'. He was sad to leave, to join foster parents, 'despite the shame of the workhouse'. 'Every Christmas', said another, 'the police used to come round and give you a voucher. That voucher was for my sister and I to get a pair of shoes from the Co-op in BURLEIGH Street. When you got there you could only have these sort of boots.' Another remembers the boots and that 'everyone knew where you'd got them.' (See H. P. Stokes, *Cambridge Parish Workhouses*, 1911, and Bridget Barclay-Munro and Helen Cook, *From Workhouse to Housework*, Cambridge City Council Arts Team, 1991.)

Philip [MAGRATH] is the name of a member of the Chartists, a working-class movement born out of the high unemployment and the Poor Law Amendments of 1834, whose effects have just been described above. The Chartists demanded universal manhood suffrage, equal electoral districts, vote by ballot, payment of Parliament members and abolition of the property qualifications for membership, all of which have since been voted into law, and annual Parliaments, which has not. The movement was not popular in Cambridge, where M'Grath (so spelt by the diarist Josiah Chater) was expected to come from London to address a meeting on 5 April 1848, but failed to appear. The *Cambridge Chronicle* reported that a man had been stationed on

Market Hill with a petition for the Charter (which gained nationally five and a half million signatures, some duplicated), but failed to interest much more than a few schoolboys, who scribbled their names repeatedly. This, the paper satirically remarked, was no doubt the reason for Magrath's absence. Some other Magrath may have been intended in the naming of this avenue.

The British Empire

Queen Victoria was designated Empress of India in 1876 and loyal Cambridge named streets for parts of the Empire just around that time: MADRAS for India, HOBART for Australia, NATAL for South Africa, MONTREAL for Canada. In the same cluster are remembered the SUEZ Canal (not part of the Empire, but vital to its existence) opened in 1869, Britain buying shares in 1875, CYPRUS, occupied by the British in 1878, and MALTA, occupied by Indian troops in 1878 (moved there by Britain to forestall Russian aggression).

[MARMORA] Road in the same cluster has no connection with the Empire, and could be a mis-spelling of the Sea of Marmara, though this too is not connected.

Whether [AUCKLAND] Road was meant to refer to the city in New Zealand is not clear. WELLINGTON and NAPIER, both in New Zealand, are also names of generals, and CHRISTCHURCH is named after the church, designed by Ambrose Poynter, dedicated in 1839, before the New Zealand name was likely to have been known. *Bishop* Auckland is a town in England. New Town (beyond the Catholic Church) was known as New Zealand prior to 1822, perhaps being at that time a remote place.

Coprolite mining

Mining for coprolite, often a name for fossilised dinosaur dung, but here mostly ammonites, was partly due to a member of the DE FREVILLE family, who bought land in Harston for the purposes of extracting the nodules.

Coprolite, used for the world's first chemical fertiliser, and involving the first large-scale open-cast mining in the British Isles, was mined from Abington north-eastwards as far as Wicken and Soham, in the period 1850–1919. There was a rush to mine it in the 1870s, but a decline later in the decade due to US and South American exports of phosphates followed by a brief revival in 1914–18, for making munitions. In 1881 coprolite was mined on the site of the present New Hall, near the West end of LATHAM Road and on Coldham's Common. In the county it caused 'one of the greatest upheavals of the landscape of Cambridgeshire of modern times', observable clearly from the air. Many Irish navvies, who had worked on the railways, found employment in this activity. (See Richard Grove, *The Cambridgeshire Coprolite Mining Rush*, 1976, and B. O'Connor, *The Dinosaurs on Coldham's Common. The Story of Cambridge's Coprolite Industry*, 1998.)

Coal, corn and iron

The tranquil scene outside Darwin College's river-front was once crowded with barges. The house later owned by the Darwins was erected in 1793 by Patrick BEALES who in 1785 bought the site and the area round it, in the corrupt days of MORTLOCK, for a very small payment. (Beales Way in

Chesterton is probably named in memory of a member of the family who was allocated land in the Chesterton Inclosure of 1840.) He developed the barge traffic on the Cam, owning all but one of the wharves on the branch of the river from Queens' to Newnham Mill. Old pictures of the Backs show barges being towed by horses walking on a raised path in the middle of the river, since there was no towpath through college grounds. (See John K. Wilson and Alan H. Faulkner, *Fenland Barge Traffic*, Robert Wilson, 1972.) Edward Fitzgerald of Trinity College, who lived at 20 King's Parade (see the plaque on the wall) wrote in *Euphranor* (1815) of the 'sluggish current' of the Cam, 'which seem'd indeed fitter for the slow merchandise of coal, than to wash the walls and flow through the groves of Academe'. Selling seed-corn and coal to farmers, Patrick BEALES junior prospered until 1845 when the railway arrived in Cambridge, and river traffic declined. Coal continued to be brought by barge until 1920, and the firm of Austin Beales delivered it until the 1950s.

Samuel BEALES, brother of Patrick, was Quartermaster of the Cambridgeshire Yeomanry Cavalry in 1801, formed to resist Napoleon, but there was no great enthusiasm for it, and it suspended operations when numbers fell to twenty-two. (See BURLEIGH, pp. 55–6.) Edmund BEALES, son of Samuel, was a liberal reformer who championed Polish refugees and manhood suffrage, organising Garibaldi's visit to England.

The brother-in-law of Patrick Beales junior was SWANN HURRELL (1816–97), who saved him from bankruptcy but not from family disgrace, for in 1869 his son Patrick absconded. He had overdrawn his account by £6,000 or £7,000 at Mortlock's Bank, having made illicit use of the Corporation Seal while he was Borough Treasurer. Both Patrick junior and Swann Hurrell were Mayors. Jane Swann Hurrell is commemorated in Great St Mary's.

In the mid-nineteenth century King's College Chapel stood between horse-drawn barges and a tall factory chimney belonging to the iron foundry, destroyed by fire in 1846, occupying the site of today's Marks and Spencer's by the market. Here at least some part of the old SILVER STREET bridge was cast in 1841. Swann Hurrell owned only one of four foundries. He was the nephew and successor of Charles FINCH, the last of a family of ironmongers whose foundry since 1688 had been on the site of the present St John's College Chapel and Master's Lodge. William Finch, who died in 1762, is commemorated in a fine tablet with broken pediment in Great St Mary's, praising him for his 'Great Probity in Business, and Benevolence to the Poor'. Finch's Walk lay alongside Hobson's Conduit beyond Brooklands Avenue. The Finches were one of the important Cambridge families, as was Hurrell, whose gentlemanly house at 30 THOMPSON'S Lane (next door to Edward Beales at no. 29) is a mark of his wealth. A later foundry was that of David Simons, who established it around 1872 in Bermuda Lane off Histon Road. This was later renamed Foundry Road and finally in 1900 BERMUDA Road.

Iron bridges made by Finch include the one at MAGDA-LENE Street (the main section cast in Derby), and one on the Backs belonging to St John's College. Three by HURRELL – bearing his name – at BROOKSIDE and the Botanic Garden are a pleasing feature of TRUMPINGTON Road. Iron posts and bollards still remain elsewhere. (See Ken Alger *et al.*, *Cambridge Iron Founders*, Cambridge Industrial Archaeology Society, 1996, and R. Lister, *Hammer and Hand – An Essay on the Iron Works in Cambridge*, Cambridge University Press Christmas book, 1969, also Margaret Keynes, *A House by the River*, 1984.)

Another corn merchant like the Beales was John Horner

Brand MARIS, born 1839 at Hinxton. He was for twelve years a County Alderman, and had agricultural interests. He was very likely present when the CORN EXCHANGE was opened in 1874. Maris House in Maris Lane dates from *c.* 1800. There are nineteenth-century tombs to the Maris family in Trumpington Church. 'Maris Piper' potatoes may have been named in connection with one of them.

Brewers

The coming of the railway to Cambridge in 1845 must have caused the extraordinarily large number of breweries here, of which there were forty around 1880, though this was partly due to the fine barley and suitable water available. These breweries often supplied a pub on adjoining premises, as the new 'Ancient Druids' near the Grafton Centre still does. The large number of such breweries in the rapidly expanding Mill Road area supplied the railway workers and manual labourers in that district. But there were breweries in the centre too, supplying beer to town and gown in MAGDALENE Street, THOMPSON'S Lane, HOBSON Street and TRINITY Streets. 'We have ourselves quaffed no small quantity of this inspiring beverage', wrote the university compilers of the eighteenth-century *Gradus ad Cantabrigiam.*

The brewers were often also prominent in town politics. The BEALES family were not only corn merchants, using their barges to bring barley for their malthouses in MALTING Lane (earlier Ffroshlake Weye, from a small stream where frogs abounded). Patrick Beales was on the Beer Committee for the Coronation Feast of 1838, supplying nine barrels of beer, as did many other brewers. Barnet William BEALES, born in 1828, owner of PANTON Brewery, was Lieutenant-Colonel of the Volunteer Corps, Trustee of All Saints Parochial Committee, Guardian of the Poor, Overseer of the Improvement Commission, Town Councillor, Alderman, County Councillor and Income Tax Commissioner. His son Albert Edward took over the brewery in the early 1890s, shortly before his father suffered serious head injuries from being knocked over by a large dog. Alderman William Henry APTHORPE (1808–84) was awarded land in the Barnwell Inclosure and owned the Victoria Brewery in what is now NAPIER Street; his son of the same name (b. 1834) owned also the Albion Brewery in CORONATION Street. The EKIN Brewery in MAGDALENE Street is reputed to have been founded in 1780, and was apparently owned by William Ekin, Mayor in 1855–6, from 1834. His son Augustus Goodman Ekin seems to have taken over the running from 1864 to 1888.

Among many other brewers were the NUTTER family, with premises in Trumpington Street and the Beehive Brewery in King Street, who owned many pubs as well as the King's Mill and Bishop's Mill in MILL Lane, but went bankrupt in 1842. Frederick BAILEY lived and had offices in Newmarket Road, and the Star Brewery in the same road, where brewing ceased in 1972. His large group of stables was approached through the brewer's yard in AUCKLAND Road. His tomb is in Christ Church opposite. His son Harold Barber Bailey was Alderman, Mayor in 1923–4, County Councillor and owner of PANTON Brewery and GRANTA Brewery. John William PAMPLIN owned the GWYDIR Brewery in 1883–8. The SWANN family is represented here by the brewer Frederick Swann, who owned the Rodney Brewery at 95 EAST Road; Swann Brothers remained there for many years as lime burners, sand and gravel dealers and general builders' merchants.

In MALTING Lane there is still a building where malt was prepared. The work there was dangerous to health. 'The humid atmosphere, the dust coming up from the dry barley before it was laid on the kiln floor' caused lung trouble. (F. T. Unwin, *Pimbo and Jenny in Old Cambridge*, 1978.) Work continued twenty-four hours a day in order to keep up the 'turning' routine. Men stuck it out for fear of unemployment. (MALT-STERS Way refers to the name of a former pub, later called 'The Bleeding Heart', which belonged to the Rowell family.)

LION Yard is named after the old Lion Hotel, which stood in Petty Cury until the shopping centre was developed. The apparently emaciated lion came from a hotel in Woburn, where it stood flat against a wall. The ROSE (and Crown) was also a coaching hotel, knocked down in 1919/20, but well known to Samuel Pepys.

JOHN CLARKE's name is given to the houses behind the Milton Arms, meant for retired publicans. He was managing director of the brewers, Greene King. The houses were built by the East Anglia Licensed Victuallers National Homes Edinburgh Estate in 1979 and opened on 3 June 1980 by the President C. E. Guinness, Esq., and the Chairman A. J. Sorrell, Esq.

KING Street was celebrated for the 'King Street Run', a trial of drinking ability in which undergraduates (mostly) ran from one pub to another, downing a pint each time, attempting to achieve the fastest run. It was formerly the name of what is now HOBSON Street, while what is now King Street was called Wall's Lane.

HARVEST Way is named after Harvest Ale, brewed by Greene King, whose store was nearby.

WHYMAN was the name of the owners of the Three Tuns at the top of Castle Hill, where Dick Turpin was said to hide.

ROSEMARY Lane appears to have been named after the Rosemary Branch public house. (The pub is named but not the lane on the OS map of 1904.)

The names of the beers are a pleasure in themselves: 'Oatmeal Stout', 'Nourishing Stout', 'Champion Beers', 'Indian Bitter Ales' (of a type provided for the troops in India) must have brought town and gown together, if not always amicably. For a name, nothing could beat the brew at the Coronation Feast: 'Sam Moore's regular, right-sort, Head-strong, Out-and-out, Strong-bodied, Ram-jam, Come-it-strong, Lift-me-up, Knock-me-down, How d'ye like it, Ge-nu-ine Midsummer-Green Stingo', of which a gallon was offered with a new hat to all competitors in a Grinning Match, a pair of velveteen trousers and a 'New Wipe' being awarded to the winner with 'the ugliest phiz'. (See R. J. Flood, *Cambridge Breweries*, 1987.)

Trams and buses

Tramways for horse-drawn trams were opened on 28 October 1880, on a route from the railway station via STATION Road, HILLS Road, REGENT Street, ST ANDREW'S Street, stopping at Christ's College. There were six trams, one every fifteen minutes. In November 1880 a branch from HYDE PARK Corner (apparently named after the one in London) via LENS-FIELD Road and TRUMPINGTON Street as far as the Market was added, and another from the Corner to EAST Road. The competition with motor-buses ended in 1914 with the winding-up of the Cambridge Street Tramways Co. for non-payment of rates. This was said, no doubt unfairly, to have been greeted with thanks by motor-cyclists. Certainly some passengers were concerned that the tram might overturn at the sharp bend by Great St Mary's. The wheels were expected to leave the track there. (See S. L. Swingle, *The Cambridge Street Tramways*, The Oakwood Press, 1972.) Horse-buses began in 1896 but ended in 1902. Motor-buses began in 1905, but many went to France as troop-carriers in 1914. They ran again in 1918, when the speed-limit was still twelve miles per hour. (See Mark Seal, *Cambridge Buses*, 1978, and Enid Porter, *Victorian Cambridge*, 1975, pp. 194–211.)

Nineteenth-century historians, antiquaries and lawyers

The major historians of this period begin with Thomas [CARLYLE] (1795–1881), essayist and author of histories of Frederick the Great and the French Revolution. He had no connection with Cambridge, but may have been meant when the street was named. (In 1851 he wrote, it is true, a biography of James Sterling of Trinity Hall. An alternative is Joseph Carlyle (1759–1804), a graduate of Trinity and Fellow of Queens', Professor of Arabic.) His powerful moral sense links curiously with his creed, derived from German philosophy, that everything is good that accords with the laws of the universe. His style has been called 'clottish', his teaching 'cloudy'. 'He had', said Herbert Spencer, 'a daily secretion of curses which he had to vent on somebody or something.' Yet W. H. Hudson praised him for making us 'feel with him the supreme claims of the moral life'.

Lord ACTON (1834–1902) would have achieved greater fame had he published more. His sobriety and modesty contrasts with that of Carlyle and Macaulay. A Roman Catholic, he had been unable to study or at any rate proceed to a degree at Cambridge (see SYLVESTER, p. 78), but, after the Test Act, became a Fellow of Trinity and Regius Professor of History, recognised abroad by such historians as Ranke. His most misquoted saying is 'Power tends to corrupt and absolute power corrupts absolutely.' In his eyes the law of human rights was a necessity to any moral form of government. He wrote little, read a book a day, it is said, and collected a huge library, now in the University Library's Acton Room. To Cardinal Manning he was 'all vanity'. To Lytton Strachey, in *Eminent Victorians*, he was 'that life-long enthusiast for liberty, that almost hysterical reviler of priestcraft and persecution', who 'wore his Rome with a difference'. In a letter Acton wrote 'I think our [historical] studies ought to be all but purposeless. They want to be pursued with chastity like mathematics.' The *Cambridge Modern History* in many volumes was due to his leadership. Yet his biographer in the DNB says that 'except in the actual investigation of the bare facts no historian is less impartial and more personal in his judgements than Acton appears in the volume on "The French Revolution"'. In this he wrote, criticising historians, 'The strong man with the dagger is followed by the weaker man with the sponge. First the criminal who slays, then the sophist who defends the slayer.'

Samuel Roffey [MAITLAND] (1792–1866), educated at St John's and Trinity, wrote about the Albigensian heretics, the Dark Ages and the Reformation. His better known grandson,

Frederic William Maitland (1850–1906), was a graduate and honorary Fellow of Trinity, and Downing Professor of the Laws of England. His principal work was the study of the history of English law, especially medieval, but he was keenly interested in Cambridge local history. He was an ardent alpinist.

Robert WILLIS (1800–75) of Caius, Jacksonian Professor of Experimental Philosophy, is specially remembered for his classic, *The Architectural History of the University of Cambridge*, 1886, added to by John Willis Clark.

Edwin GUEST (1800–80), Master of Caius, was practically the founder of the Philological Society, and of the study of Roman British history. An 'unvacillating' conservative and an evangelical churchman, he did everything to promote the interests of his college.

Sir Adolphus William WARD (1837–1924) was Master of Peterhouse, Vice-Chancellor and editor-in-chief of the *Cambridge Modern History*. He also wrote extensively on history, especially in relation to literature.

Nineteenth-century scientists

Nineteenth-century Cambridge was not distinguished for science until Prince ALBERT as Chancellor began in the middle of the century reforms inspired by his awareness of how far the University lagged behind German universities. NEWTON's legacy had been consumed without regard for Continental discoveries, but two leaders in non-mathematical fields are commemorated in street-names. Sir Humphry DAVY (1778–1829), inventor of the safety-lamp for miners, resided at Jesus in 1804, was assistant to the great Faraday and was a friend of

COLERIDGE, but his main work was on gases and chemical elements and was done elsewhere. He nearly died in an attempt to inhale carburetted hydrogen gas. Adam SEDGWICK (1785–1873) was a geologist who preceded but helped to create the Victorian period of great enthusiasm for his subject. He had no knowledge of geology when appointed, but undertook to 'get it up', later inspiring many younger men to devote themselves to the subject, including one of the greatest scientists the world has known. His field-classes involved excursions on horseback, as many as seventy participating. (No friend of women's university education, unlike Henry SIDGWICK, he spoke of women students as 'nasty, forward minxes', yet he was a liberal, in many other ways broad-minded and humane.)

Charles DARWIN (1809–82) attended few lectures while an undergraduate at Christ's, although he was always grateful for those by the Director of the Botanic Garden, John Stevens Henslow (after whom a Walk in the Garden is named). 'His lectures [in 1828] were universally popular', Darwin wrote, 'and as clear as daylight', adding that Henslow kept open house once a week, where 'I have listened to the great men of those days, conversing on all sorts of subjects, with the most varied and brilliant powers.' This was clearly more useful than the official curriculum, yet still a University education. It was Henslow who suggested to Darwin he should read geology, which he did, in a postgraduate term, and introduced him to SEDGWICK, with whom Henslow had made a field-trip to the Isle of Wight. It was also Henslow who recommended Darwin for the post as naturalist on the famous voyage of the *Beagle*, from which so much of the material for his ideas on evolution was gathered. The claim that Cambridge did nothing for Darwin, still sometimes heard, thus needs alteration. (In the late 1840s Henslow also urged the mining of coprolite, with great effect on Cambridge industry and population.)

Sir FRANCIS DARWIN (1848–1925), the son of Charles Darwin, was at Trinity as an undergraduate and at Christ's as a Fellow. He worked on vegetable physiology and published his father's letters. Sir Horace DARWIN (1851–1928), youngest son of Charles, made an impact on Cambridge life by his Cambridge Scientific Instrument Company founded in 1881, which developed a seismograph, instruments for temperature control, paper chart recorders, a galvanometer and an electro-cardiograph, and produced and marketed in 1913 the cloud chambers of C. T. R. Wilson, leading to RUTHERFORD'S 'splitting' of the atom. This firm provided employment for highly skilled Cambridge men such as Frank DOGGETT who had no university qualifications. Sir Horace was Mayor, 1896–7, having set himself the task of bringing University and Town together. 'Ida' DARWIN, his wife, founded with others the Cambridgeshire Voluntary Association for Mental Welfare in 1908. The hospital at Fulbourn is named after her. (See David H. Clark, *The Story of a Mental Hospital. Fulbourn 1858–1953*). Sir Horace himself with others installed a school for mentally backward boys in the Old Rectory, Girton. (See M. J. G. Cattermole and A. F. Wolfe, *Horace Darwin's Shop. A History of the Cambridge Scientific Instrument Company 1878–1968*, Adam Hilger, Bristol and Boston, 1987.)

Thomas Vernon Wollaston (1822–78) was a friend of Darwin who wrote a book *On the Variation of Species* published in 1856, three years before Darwin's *Origin of Species* was published. However, the street bearing this name is in a cluster of Caius street-names, and William Hyde WOLLASTON (1766–1828), of Caius and Trinity, physiologist, chemist and physicist, was surely intended. He invented a method for producing pure platinum and welding it into vessels, as well as the Camera Lucida, which led to the invention of photography. He also proved that electricity, whether produced by galvanic action or by friction, is of the same nature. Yet another of this name, A. F. R. ('Sandy') Wollaston should surely be remembered, if not originally meant to be. He was 'explorer, naturalist and medical officer in Lapland, Central Africa, New Guinea, Colombia, and on the Everest Expedition of 1921, ending as Fellow and Tutor, only to be murdered in 1930 by a demented freshman', as the historian of King's Christopher Morris relates.

The Revd Henry ('Ben') LATHAM (1821–1902) published on geometry, and devotional works, but gave himself above all else to the interests of Trinity Hall, where a building is named after him. He was Senior Tutor 1856–85 and Master 1888–1902. Sir Henry Dickens said of him, 'If ever a tutor made a College, Ben Latham made Trinity Hall . . . He was somewhat odd in appearance, tall, slightly stooping, rather gaunt and with a curious halting kind of walk.' He built the house called SOUTHACRE in 1880 and gave his name to the adjacent road, where the Vice-Chancellor now resides. He was devoted to undergraduates, though in the end he became forgetful, and once famously said 'I believe – in Pontius Pilate (pause) – no, I don't.' (Was this a slip while reciting the Creed?) He was celebrated for his knowledge of Cambridge butterflies and byways and his shrewd Stock Exchange tips, but found it difficult to distinguish ladies – 'they are all so much alike'. He died in the evening after being driven to see the college row in the May Races.

Latham preferred Chaucer to all other poets, which may be the reason for the naming of CHAUCER Road. It was quickly occupied by married dons taking advantage of the legislation of 1882 allowing them to marry. Soon after came businessmen, Mayors and Aldermen, in 1888 the great cricketer Ranjitsinhji, at no. 1, and the exiled daughter of Stalin, Svetlana Peters, at no. 12. EDWINSTOWE Close or Drive is named after a house on this road (and there is a village of this name near Mansfield). (See Jane M. Renfrew *et al.*, *Rus in Urbe, Chaucer Road and Latham Road. The History of Two Rural Roads in Cambridge*, Solachra, Cambridge, 1996.)

By the end of the nineteenth century Cambridge was already what it remains today, a foremost university in the world for mathematics. James Joseph SYLVESTER (1814–97) of St John's had a distinguished career in America and as Savilian Professor in Oxford. His contributions to algebra and number theory were important. He is also remembered for not being allowed to proceed to his degree for about forty years after he had taken the Tripos. As a Jew, he was allowed, as were a few others who were not members of the Church of England, to attend courses but not to proceed to degrees until after the Test Act of 1872 abolished the discrimination. Women suffered under the same discrimination even longer, until 1948.

William Thomson, Baron KELVIN (1824–1907), of Peterhouse, was looked upon as one of the greatest living authorities on all scientific matters. He evolved the theory that forms the basis of wireless telegraphy, and superintended the laying of the cable across the Atlantic, showed the possibility of utilising the power of Niagara in generating electricity, worked at the mathematical theory of magnetism, reformed the mariner's compass and invented a machine for predicting tides. He helped to found the University Music Society. Sir Ambrose Fleming says of him that he could sit at a meal, with a faraway look in his eyes and yet still attend apparently to what was going on around him. At lunch one day when plans for an afternoon excursion were being discussed, he suddenly looked up and said 'At what time does the dissipation of energy begin?'

James CLERK MAXWELL (1831–79) of Peterhouse and later a Fellow of Trinity led the simplest of lives. 'I have regularly set up shop now above the wash-house at the gate, in a garret', he wrote in 1848, 'I have an old door set on two barrels, and two chairs, of which one is safe, and a skylight above, which will slide up and down.' This convinced him later that many of the greatest problems in physics can be solved with comparatively simple apparatus. One of his great contributions as the first Professor of Experimental Physics was a brilliant essay on the rings of the planet Saturn; he also published on the kinetic theory of gases and on colour-blindness, but above all on electricity and magnetism: Marconi acknowledged his debt to him. Einstein said of him that his conception of Reality as represented by continuous fields, not capable of any mechanical interpretation, was 'the most profound and the most fruitful that physics has experienced since the time of Newton'. He was an ardent Christian, but strongly against university education for women.

Yet another scientist of great distinction was John William Strutt, third Baron RAYLEIGH (1842–1919), Fellow of Trinity and Professor of Experimental Physics after Clerk Maxwell – also brother-in-law of the Prime Minister, Lord Balfour. He too was concerned among many other things with electricity, but his greatest single contribution was the discovery of the element argon, in 1894, developing the largely forgotten work of Henry CAVENDISH more than a century earlier. (Argon is used in gas-filled electric light bulbs, in radio tubes and Geiger counters, and for arc-welding certain metals.) For his role in this discovery he received in 1904 the Nobel Prize for Physics. However, his researches covered almost the whole field of exact science, resulting in 446 papers, at the rate of about nine a year. His lucid explanations made even the most abstruse subjects appear simple.

In 1908 Rayleigh became Chancellor of the University. He had a life-long interest in psychical research, as did many scholars of his generation. He was an enthusiast for 'real' tennis.

Nineteenth-century bishops and clergy

More nineteenth-century Bishops were honoured by having streets named after them than in any other century and they conform to no stereotype. William Lort MANSEL (1753–1820), Bishop of Bristol, Master of Trinity, was a wit and writer of epigrams, as became a cleric of the eighteenth century, although the epigrams quoted by W. W. Rouse Ball lack punch. It was perhaps he who wrote the verses about a garden made by a master of Trinity Hall, though they are also ascribed to PORSON:

> If you would know the mind of little Jowett
> This little garden does a little show it.

He respected the college rule prohibiting dogs by carrying his – called Isaac – whenever he crossed Great Court with it. (R. A. Butler's dog, during his Mastership, was deemed a cat.) He was a man of the world, who during the French Revolution wanted to live on good terms even with 'Jacobin' Fellows, but found it hard to put up with BYRON'S verses suggesting his pomposity:

High in the midst surrounded by his peers
Magnus his ample front sublime uprears;
Placed on his throne of state he seems a god,
Whilst sophs and freshmen tremble at his word.

HARVEY GOODWIN (1818–91) of Caius, Bishop of
Carlisle, by contrast, founded a school in Victoria Road. The
Waifs and Strays Society between 1896 and 1920 used the former
Industrial School buildings for the school for boys, named after
him. A prolific publisher of theology and sermons, he also wrote
on elementary dynamics. He published his autobiography pri-
vately. He was the first principal of the Cambridge Working
Men's College, at which dons acted as tutors.

George Elwes CORRIE (1793–1885), Master of Jesus, was
a staunch conservative and Evangelical, strongly opposed to
reform that would allow others than Church of England
men – or women – entry to the University, and equally opposed
to dissent of any kind, whether Papist or Protestant. 'The last
ditch', it has been said of him, 'was his spiritual home', and
he inveighed against tourists coming by train on the
Sabbath. He was President of the Architectural Society, yet
although William Morris and Co. decorated the chapel during
his Mastership, in his biography by M. Holroyd (1890) there is
no mention of this notable event.

Harvey Goodwin wrote a memoir of Charles Frederick
MACKENZIE (1825–62), Bishop of Central Africa, of Caius
(which he joined after resigning from St John's, where, as a
Scotsman, he was debarred from a Fellowship). Mackenzie
joined Livingstone in freeing slaves from African owners, and
promoted equality between blacks and whites in Christian
congregations. In his enthusiasm he helped one tribe against
another, which resulted in the burning down of a village. He

died of fever at Malo. Livingstone erected a cross over his grave. (See Owen Chadwick, *Mackenzie's Grave*, 1959.)

George Augustus SELWYN (1809–78) was also an explorer. He visited the whole of New Zealand in 1847, the Pacific Islands in 1847–8 and became primate of New Zealand in 1841. He was a keen critic of the unjust and reckless procedures of the English land companies, but was misunderstood by the Maoris themselves. In the war of 1855 he worked hard to provide Christian ministrations to the troops on both sides. Selwyn College was erected by public subscription in his memory.

William EMERY, another Caian, named in the street next to MACKENZIE, was Archdeacon of Ely (1864–1907). He took a leading part in providing Ely with pure water and initiated the Volunteer movement by starting the Cambridge Rifle Club in 1859. This Club was formed during a wave of patriotic fervour which had just swept the country. After the Indian Mutiny of 1857 it was realised that a volunteer, part-time force for home defence was needed to relieve the regular army, and this eventually became the Territorial Army. When the Club's rifle range was opened at Grange Road, ROSS, champion of England, fired the initial shots. The street named after Ross once led to the old butts on Coldham's Common, which stretched from east to west over 800 yards.

GELDART Street is named after James William Geldart (1785–1876), Fellow and Vice-Master of Trinity Hall and rector of Kirk Deighton, Yorkshire, who owned the land in that area.

Two brothers, both of Corpus Christi, are remembered in PEROWNE Street. Edward Henry (1826–1906) was Master of the College, which in his time was largely a training-ground for Evangelicals hoping to be ordained, and often to become missionaries. John James Stewart Perowne (1823–1904), Fellow, became Bishop of Worcester, and was later a Fellow of Trinity.

Henry Richards LUARD (1825–91) was the kind of man often thought of as a typical Victorian don: a Tory, High Churchman, opponent of the right of dons to marry (though among the first to do so), his great ambition was to be a Fellow of Trinity, which he achieved. He bitterly regretted innovations in the University, and vehemently opposed them. He was Registrary and Vicar of Great St Mary's. Thanks to him the gallery over the chancel where heads of houses sat, known for that reason as Golgotha, 'the place of skulls' was pulled down. He had a 'stately courtesy' as well as a 'vivacious impulsiveness', and despite his dislike of Garibaldi was always willing to allow others their point of view. (See J. Willis Clark, *Old Friends at Cambridge and Elsewhere*, 1900.)

William BATESON (1812–81) was Master of St John's, head of the liberal party in academic matters, and a promoter of the higher education of women. He had acute judgement, and a remarkably sweet and tender character.

The first vicar of ST LUKE'S Church, in 1881, was George HALE of Sidney Sussex. He served largely at his own expense, usually assisted by two curates, and died exhausted in 1889. The street was previously called Queen Street. In the same neighbourhood, the Rev. Dr C. E. SEARLE, Master of Pembroke 1880–1902, who had close associations with St Luke's, is also remembered. (See also STRETTON, p. 2.)

Architects

James [ESSEX] (1722–84), the architect (who has more Cambridge connections than the many Earls of Essex have – although the Elizabethan Earl, Robert Devereux, was Chancellor of the University) designed the west front of

Emmanuel. He was by far the most popular architect with the colleges in the eighteenth century. He also restored and altered Ely Cathedral and put up the four spires on the central tower of Lincoln Cathedral. (See *The Ingenious Mr Essex, Architect, 1722–1784*, Exhibition Catalogue, Fitzwilliam Museum, Cambridge, 1984.) He is buried in St Botolph's Church.

Charles Robert COCKERELL (1788–1863) designed the Taylorian Building in Oxford, and the Ashmolean Museum adjoining. In Cambridge he made a design for a new University Library, involving the destruction of the Old Schools, but only the Squire Law Library, now Caius College Library, was built. He took over the interior decoration of the Fitzwilliam Museum, begun by Basevi and completed by E. M. Barry. Less well known was Basil CHAMPNEYS (1842–1935), who designed much of Newnham College – surely his masterpiece – and Selwyn Divinity School.

[HUMPHREYS] Road can scarcely be intended to remember Charles Humfrey, Mayor in 1837–38, and architect, or Sir George Humphry. (See 'Hospitals', p. 97.)

[WILKIN] is conceivably a mis-spelling of the name of William Wilkins (1778–1839) who lived in LENSFIELD Road and designed the screen, library, Provost's Lodge, bridge and dining hall of King's, the main layout of Downing, New Court at Trinity, and the façade, New Court and Chapel of Corpus Christi, as well as the National Gallery and many other buildings throughout England. He is buried in the chapel of Corpus Christi, to which he donated fine Renaissance stained glass. (See R. W. Liscombe, *William Wilkins 1778–1839*, 1980.) Wilkin Street is between the streets named after Corpus Christi men, Mawson and Tenison. However, the name Wilkin is that of some parishioners of St Barnabas Church in the same area.

Northampton Street

[BRANDON] Place was first built *c.* 1830. Alterations to St Bene't's Church were made in 1853 from designs by J. R. Brandon, and R. Brandon directed work on St Edwards's church 1858–60. One of these – if they are not the same man – could have built the street also. This is also the name of a town in Norfolk.

The 'Kite' area

The area between EAST Road, PARKSIDE, EMMANUEL Road and MAIDS' CAUSEWAY was known because of its shape as the Kite, during the long agitation of the 1970s against the project for the GRAFTON Centre. In this area, Charles Humfrey's garden is marked by ORCHARD Street, and perhaps [ELM] Street. Also in the neighbourhood was a market-garden known as the Garden of EDEN, which gave rise to the names ADAM AND EVE Street and PARADISE Street. It may be argued that [PROSPECT] Row, being close to these, should bring to mind the lines from the once well-known hymn 'From Greenland's Icy Mountains', contrasting the paradise of Nature with human wickedness: 'every prospect pleases, and only man is vile'. The author, Bishop Heber, died in 1826, before the street was built, probably unaware that the prospect in this part of Cambridge was far from paradisal. (COVENT GARDEN, just outside the 'Kite', also commemorates a market-garden, named after the London street.) Common land had been enclosed everywhere and sold off, with disruptive social effects. (See Christopher Taylor, *The Cambridgeshire Landscape*, 1973, p. 182.) The Barnwell Inclosure Act of 1807 had led to speculative building in the whole area, which by the middle of the century had become a slum, rife with disease caused by inadequate or non-existent drainage, ventilation and water supply. (See Michael Murphy, *Cambridge Newspapers and Opinion 1780–1850*, 1977.) The Revd William Leeke, who had been the youngest ensign at Waterloo (but the street named after him has been demolished) made efforts to improve conditions by starting a Sunday school, which led eventually to the foundation of an elementary school in [MELBOURNE] Place, now Parkside Community College. This was against strong opposition to educating working-class children, even as late as 1913, partly from the Mayor, Councillor Francis. Today, however, the whole area is gentrified, being close to the centre, and professors live where their servants once lived. The working-class people have moved out to ARBURY. (See Rosemary Gardiner, *An Epoch Making School*, Parkside Community College, Cambridge, 1988.)

Sport

Football in Cambridge owed a lot to undergraduates at Trinity who in 1848 formulated a complete set of laws. These came into conflict with laws closer to those of rugby, including one that 'no player was to be held, and hacked at the same time', which Cambridge men opposed. ABBEY United, now a professional club known as Cambridge United, is believed to have begun in a match under a street-lamp in STANLEY Road in 1912. This was only a few hundred yards from Abbey Road, in the Abbey Ward, which presumably gave rise to the name. The Revd W. Carr, curate of the Abbey Church, was the club's first president, elected soon after the end of the First World War.

(See Paul M. Daw, *United in Endeavour. A History of Abbey United/Cambridge United F.C. 1912–1988*, 1988.)

The LENTS and the MAYS are the names of the University rowing races, the so-called 'Bumps' on the Cam. Owing to the narrowness of the river boats start at an interval from one another, each trying to bump the boat in front. Successful crews change places with the bumped crews on the following day, for four days, beginning in the new positions each year. Steve FAIRBAIRN (1862–1938) is remembered in the Fairbairn races, and for the great help he gave to Cambridge rowing, especially to Jesus College. The memorial marking the distance of one mile from the start of the University Boat Race on the Thames commemorates him as founder of the Head of the River race.

Jack Hobbs (Sir John Berry Hobbs, 1882–1963), the cricketer and great batsman, lived as a boy in RIVAR Place. He first played in county cricket for Cambridgeshire in 1904, and scored 197 centuries in first-class cricket. The Hobbs Pavilion on Parker's Piece is named after him. 'Rivar' comes from River House in SLEAFORD Street, owned by a man known as 'Miser' KINGSTON, a recluse with a long beard who frightened children. (See 'Landowners', p. 133.)

TENNIS COURT Road records the court for 'real' (i.e. 'royal') tennis, existing in 1564, now demolished. Similar courts, though more recent, are still in use at Grange Road. (Lawn tennis dates from the 1870s.)

Builders and developers

Builders and developers have a better chance of influencing the naming of streets than many others. Rattee and Kett have provided stone for colleges and such places as Westminster Abbey since 1843, as well as repairing and building generally. PURBECK marble is obtained by them from a quarry near CORFE in Dorset. The names are given to streets near their premises. (See Anna de Salvo, *Kett of Cambridge, an Eminent Victorian and his Family*, National Extension College Trust Ltd, 1993.) [ANCASTER] is another well-known quarry, whose stone was used for St John's Chapel. (The Duchess of Ancaster was Thomas PANTON's daughter.) Also founded in Victorian times was Kidman and Sons Ltd, in 1876. CHARLES Street was named after the elder son of Charles Kidman, who built much of the site, and other streets were also named after members of the family, probably [DAVID], parallel to Charles Street, but not CATHARINE, named after the wife of HERBERT (THODAY), the builder. [GEORGE] Street, parallel to Herbert Street, may well also refer to a member of the Thoday family. KELSEY and KER-RIDGE are parts of the name of a well-known builder, com-memorated not only in street-names but in the name of the Sports Hall by Parker's Piece, opened in 1975. Alderman Kelsey Charles Kerridge of Cambridge City Council was Chairman of Kerridge (Cambridge) Ltd, and was sixty-one in 1969. He was a great enthusiast for all sports and became MBE in the same year.

Charles BLINCO was surveyor to the ROCK Freehold Land Society, which developed an area between Hills Road and Cherry Hinton Road, but according to another account he was a banker who bought land from the Society. [HARTINGTON] and [MARSHALL], parallel to Blinco Grove, may also have been connected with this development, but Hartington is a name connected, like CAVENDISH, with the Dukes of Devonshire, and Cavendish College preceded HOMERTON College on the site across the road; this is more likely to have been intended. [BURRELL'S] Walk may be named after a farmer from Coton, from whom the land was bought. A portrait of him is extant, wearing late eighteenth-century costume. The same man (1730–1805) may be meant by the 'linen draper of Market Hill' who used to walk to Coton this way. A tailor and robe-maker's shop in Rose Crescent was run by James Burrell in 1891. The second Baron GWYDIR was named Peter Burrell, but this is the least likely connection.

Thomas Lovell Naylor, builder, named GARRY Drive after his son, and LOVELL Road. KENDAL Way was so named because the builders, R. A. Baines and Sons, came from Kendal. NEWELL Walk was named by a developer. H. C. MOSS, builder, of Cottenham, built houses near the railway embankment in Chesterton which gives rise to 'Bank' in the street-name. COLWYN is the name of the home-town of the builders of the street.

A builder named BRADWELL was a partner of William Grumbold in work on the West Range of Clare College in 1669. A tombstone against the wall of St Andrew's Church in St Andrew's Street opposite Bradwell's Court bears the name of David Bradwell, who died, aged seventy-eight, on 24 December 1813. George Bradwell designed Victoria Homes almshouses in VICTORIA Road in 1837; of which the original block was demolished in the 1970s. Alderman Thomas Bradwell died in 1877. Before the present Court was built, Bradwell's builders yard, owned by a later David Bradwell, occupied the plot. It was demolished in 1958.

PAKENHAM Close was named by the builder, Mr Lambert, from a selection of names offered for his choice by the City

Council. There is a Pakenham near Bury St Edmund's. The first houses in HEMINGFORD Road were built by G. Smith of Hemingford Grey.

EAST Road (the Old Mill Way in the fifteenth century) was Gravel Pit Road in 1811 – the lower levels off NORFOLK Street are due to such pits.

Localities in Cambridge

Some street-names indicate places nearby, as AIRPORT, BAKERY (no longer existing), and BIGGIN near Horningsea, included in Heffers/OS map of 1995 (leading to Biggin Abbey; 'biggin' means 'building'). There is no evidence of an abbey here: the house was a summer residence of the Bishops of Ely, and has a stone range of the fourteenth century. (See N. Pevsner, *Cambridgeshire*, 1954, 2nd edn, 1970.) BROOK Lane refers to the Bin Brook, which derives its name from 'binnan', 'within' – the brook formed in part a boundary between the town and the country, the land 'within' being part of the town; BROOKLANDS is the name of a house (Brookland in 1830) by the 'Vicar's Brook' behind Newton Road; Brookland Farm occupied the land to the east; BROOKSIDE is beside Hobson's Brook, and is the most beautiful street in Cambridge. BROOK-FIELD is near the Bin Brook; BURNSIDE and BROOK-FIELDS are near Cherry Hinton Brook. [BROOKS], in a Peterhouse cluster, is probably named after W.M'I. Brooks, architect of a Peterhouse building built by the benefaction of Francis GISBORNE. CAM CAUSEWAY was intended to cross the Cam to link up with the ring road but was never completed. CAUSEWAY Passage (Causeway Court before 1904) relates to Maids' Causeway. THE FEN CAUSEWAY was built *c.* 1930, vigorously opposed by country-lovers. (See Quentin Nelson's poem, separately published, 'The Coe Fen Road'.) CHAPEL Street was named for a former Baptist Chapel, now a meeting-hall. The CORN EXCHANGE was used by farmers until the Second World War. A FAIR is still held on Midsummer Common, as it has been for nearly 800 years, though only a vestige of the commercial fair remains. CUTTER FERRY ('cutter', meaning a rowing or sailing boat, but the Cam ferries were operated eventually by chain) and FERRY Lane and Ferry Path (leading to the Fort St George in England, so named to distinguish it from one in Madras) are where ferries were the only way of crossing the river downstream from Magdalene bridge, before the Victoria bridge was built. A ferry was leased by the town to John Bruys in 1385. LOGAN is the name of a ferryman in 1854. (See M. Heron, *Ferry Path*, 1974.) The FREE SCHOOL was founded by Stephen PERSE in 1615. Before 1842 the Fitzwilliam Museum was housed in it; now the Whipple History of Science Museum occupies the Hall, or Big School. A GRANGE was an isolated farm such as existed at the present University Sports ground, near Grange Road. (Grange Drive leads to Girton Grange.) GUILDHALL Street was once Butchers' Row, the present name dating from around 1874. HALL FARM was also an isolated farm, practising arable farming. SIDNEY FARM Road is where Sidney Hall Farm still was in 1904. The land was allocated to Sidney Sussex College in the Barnwell Inclosure of 1811. WHITEHOUSE Lane was so named because it leads to a white house.

A LIMEKILN used the outcrop of chalk near Cherry Hinton. There were MANOR gardens, of which Manor Street off Jesus Lane was the eastern boundary. The MARKET has existed on its present site for centuries. MILL END was Le Mylhende as far back as 1511. The POST OFFICE moved in 1850 from 44 SIDNEY Street, to the site of the Brazen George Inn, once a hostel of Christ's College, to which it stood opposite, and finally to the corner of PETTY CURY and ST ANDREW'S Street in 1855. The RAILWAY runs close by the street named after it. The word REGATTA is used for the Town Headway Regatta. CAPSTAN and MARINER'S relate to the ferry and to the cruising boats formerly hired at BANHAM'S Yard. MISSLETON is the name of a hill off Wort's Causeway. ARCHWAY Court has its own archway.

The BROADWAY (not the one in Grantchester) stands on the site of Mill Villa, later called The Lodge, which was demolished, and the present shops built, in the 1930s, numbered separately to avoid renumbering the whole road.

FULBROOKE is named after what is called on the OS map of 1865 the Full Brook, but the original derivation, like that of *Ful*bourne, is more likely to be from the equivalent of 'fowl brook'.

PARSONAGE Street is beside an original parsonage of CHRISTCHURCH.

PRIMARY Court is named after the primary school which formerly stood here.

[DAWS] may refer to the presence of jackdaws: Coe Fen is perhaps named for such a presence, *co(o)* being Middle English for a jackdaw, but 'Cow Fen' might have been its name. Daws Lane was allocated to John Headley in the Cherry Hinton Inclosure of 1806.

There were once FOUR LAMPS at the road-junction so named.

Peas Hill

Hospitals

The area near New Addenbrooke's Hospital has several
names apparently connected with it, which are rather to be
explained because the area – of the manor that had once
belonged to Thomas MOWBRAY – belonged from 1553
onward to St Thomas's Hospital, London, or in some cases
from the Cherry Hinton Inclosure of 1806. (See 'The Survey
of St Thomas' Hospital Land in Cherry Hinton, Made by
John Tracey in 1733', in H. C. Coppock, *Over the Hills to
Cherry Hinton*, 1984, and London Metropolitan Archives
H.I./ST/E115/9 and 10.) ALMONERS Avenue refers to
the medieval name of a hospital official who gave alms. Until
recently the title was used for one who dealt with payments by
patients, and their welfare. Florence NIGHTINGALE
(1820–1910) is famous as 'The Lady with the Lamp', who
carried out reforms in the Army medical service in the Crimea,
against much opposition, and powerfully advocated similar
reforms in India. Lytton Strachey's essay on her in *Eminent
Victorians* does justice to her astonishing thrustfulness and
courage. 'What a comfort it was', said a patient in the Crimean
War, 'to see her pass. She would speak to me, and nod and
smile to as many more; but she could not do it to all, you know.
We lay there by the hundreds; but we could kiss her shadow as
it fell and lay our heads on the pillow again content.'
Associated with Florence Nightingale was Lady Mary Jane
KINNAIRD (1816–88), who sent nursing and other aid to the
wounded in the Crimea, and was one of the founders of the
Young Women's Christian Association.

TOPCLIFFE is the name of a manor in Meldreth,
Cambridgeshire, that belonged to St Thomas's.

FENDON is the name of an open field also at one time owned by St Thomas's Hospital. 'Beyond Fendon' is shown on a terrier of Hinton lands in 1733, addressed to the Governors of the Hospital. MALLETT(S) Furlong is shown on a survey of land in Teversham belonging to the hospital in 1688.

RED CROSS, however, refers not to the charitable organisation but to a cross, such as was often placed at the entrance to a town, that stood at the fork of Hills Road and Worts' Causeway. The name comes immediately from Red Cross Farm, which may have been named after such a cross; the name is recorded in the early sixteenth century, and a cross is shown at the fork on an Inclosure map of Cherry Hinton.

STRANGEWAYS refers to the laboratory named after T. S. P. Strangeways, near the same fork, founded in 1912, originally a hospital, which researches on nutrition, endocrinology, cyto-chemistry, radiobiology and microbiology. It began in HARTINGTON Grove, where a converted coal-shed proved inadequate for research. Mrs E. Dorothy Strangeways, a governor of the Perse School for Girls, may also have been intended.

Whether [ST THOMAS'S] Square is named after the hospital is not certain. It is in an area just north of the land owned by the hospital (named after St Thomas a Becket the martyr (1118–70), later after the Apostle St Thomas Didymus), but just south of the Roman Catholic school, St Bede's, which might suggest St Thomas Aquinas (1225–74) whose *Summa Theologiae* was for centuries the standard authority of the Roman Catholic Church. The next four entries are mentioned in A. Rook *et al.*, *The History of Addenbrooke's Hospital*, 1991. Sir George Edward [PAGET] (1809–92) was physician there and is the subject of a whole chapter (but see 'High Stewards',

p. 110). Sir George [HUMPHRY] (1820–96) was surgeon to the hospital; there is a chapter about him also (but see 'Architects', p. 83). William Henry DROSIER (1811–89) was his deputy, and Senior Tutor of Caius, to which he was a great benefactor. Dr Malcolm [HERON] (1918–74) set up a unit at Addenbrooke's Hospital for controlling the spread of hard drugs. As a psychiatrist he was committed to group and social therapy.

ROBINSON Way was named after David Robinson, who put up half the cost of the Rosie Maternity Hospital, three million out of six million pounds, in memory of his mother.

A poet

Lord BYRON (1788–1824) was at Trinity in 1805–8, where he read much history and fiction, boxed and swam – Byron's Pool is not far from Byron Square, though now desecrated. It is not certain he swam there. More likely is the place near Paradise Island, popular with undergraduates, where his friend C. S. Matthews was drowned in 1811, entangled by weeds. However, the Pool was known to village children as Dead Man's Hole. In 1868 it was used for washing sheep. (See F. Reeve, *Cambridge from the River*, 1977.) While at Cambridge Byron published his 'Hours of Idleness', severely criticised in the 'Edinburgh Review', and replied in 1809 with 'English Bards and Scotch Reviewers'. He challenged Hewson Clark of Emmanuel to a duel, for another adverse review of 'Hours of Idleness', but failed to find him in. (See Chainey, *A Literary History of Cambridge*, p. 26 above, for Byron's time at Cambridge.)

Brookside

Mayors

The first municipal officer of Cambridge to be called 'Mayor' was Hervey fitz Eustace Dunning, in the mid-thirteenth century. He lived in what is now called The School of Pythagoras. John [GOLDING] was Mayor in 1304, but was not intended when the street-name was given. No other relevant names occur in the list of Mayors published by J. M. Gray until 1524, when Thomas BRACKYN appears. He was also Mayor in 1539 and 1543, and represented Cambridge in Parliament between 1548 and 1552. He promoted a Bill for the paving of Cambridge, and tried to get relief from providing the full quota of twenty archers imposed upon the Town. A fishmonger, he managed to get himself appointed as purveyor of pikes to Henry VIII, which led to profitable dealings, buying fish for the king but selling much of it on the market at high prices. He disputed in 1534 the control of Stourbridge Fair, but lost to the Vice-Chancellor. His son Richard was Mayor in 1549 and also represented the Town in Parliament. Richard was a tenant of BARNWELL Priory, and enclosed some of its land after the Dissolution for his own use. Richard's son Thomas sold some of this land to Francis Ventris. Edward [THOMPSON] (Mayor 1534) may have been resident in Thompson's Lane. Thomas Ventris (1559) (who was also representative of Cambridge in Parliament in 1575) is to be remembered, as well as later people with the same name, in VENTRESS Close and Ventress Farm Court. The Ventris family continued to live in Cherry Hinton in the nineteenth and twentieth centuries. C. F. [FLETCHER] was Mayor in 1565 and 1573 but this association is unlikely to have been intended. Oliver GREENE (1594), whose name occurs in Green Street, leased the hermitage at Small Bridges (Silver Street) no doubt for the tolls to be collected there. The first SPALDING to be commemorated is Samuel (c. 1590–1669), Mayor in 1630, but several others of this name followed. His name was appended to an appeal to fortify Cambridge Castle for Parliament. He was a member of the committee for ejecting royalist clergy. His accounts as a tax collector were above suspicion – not a usual thing in his day. He was one of the 'adventurers' who undertook the drainage of the Bedford Level. W. [BISHOP] was Mayor in 1844–5, W. P. Spalding in 1908–10, A. A. Spalding in 1933–4 and 1938–39. One [NICHOLSON] was Mayor in 1659; his wife was a Quaker. Francis [FINCH] was Mayor in 1664.

Henry Pyke (1692) died a prisoner in Cambridge Castle on 9 September 1697. ([PIKE'S] Walk may be connected.) His son Joseph (1710) was in a quarrel recorded in his Diary by Alderman Newton: 'Saturday night about 10 or 11 at the Rose Taverne in Cambridge upon a quarrell betweene Alderman Thomas Fox jnr. & Joseph Pyke concerning the Towne Clarks place, the said Mr Fox with his penknife did stabb the said Joseph Pyke in his side near his belly; *but he recovered of the wound.*' The son was guilty of bribery and intimidation, doing great harm to the prestige of the Corporation. He was given Anglesey Abbey by the MP Samuel Shepherd, whose secretary he had once been. (However, a John Pyke was allocated land in Chesterton in 1840.) Thomas NUTTING was Mayor in 1723 and 1743. He was buried in St Clement's Church. James GIFFORD, Mayor in 1757, owned a house in Gifford Place. When feeling was running high over the American question he was pelted and badly hurt at election time, dying as a result a few years later in 1774, aged sixty. His son James, Mayor in 1766, was serving in North America with the 14th Foot when he was elected, but the election was made, since he could not return, only to secure the continuance in office of his predecessor. He never took up office, but served in Dominica in a punitive expedition against the Caribs. He died in 1813.

William [NORFOLK] (1769) is mentioned elsewhere, as is his son-in-law (JAMES) BURLEIGH (1770).

John MORTLOCK is the most remarkable of all Cambridge Mayors. He gained popularity by his goodwill, for example by issuing letters of credit to travellers who feared to be robbed of their cash by highwaymen if they approached the town at dusk, also by petitioning for peace with the American colonies, and for advocating a more democratic system of Parliamentary representation. But he also got all the principal posts in the Corporation into his own hands or of those he appointed, and blackmailed opponents to secure his position. He was a close ally of the Duke of RUTLAND, whose 'pocket borough' Cambridge became (see 'High Stewards', p. 115). Mortlock founded the first bank in Cambridge, alongside where Barclays Bank now stands (1780); he was Mayor in 1785, and twelve times more by 1809, while his son John Cheetham Mortlock was Mayor in 1802 and eight times more by 1820, and his son Frederick Cheetham Mortlock was Mayor in 1810 and three times more by 1816. The middle name is for once curiously appropriate. Between 1785 and 1820 the Mortlocks were Mayors almost every year. In 1784 the eldest Mortlock was MP for Cambridge but was censured by the House of Commons for underhanded dealings.

COLERIDGE records meeting John MORTLOCK on 25 September 1794 and listening to his 'damned chatter'. He was 'guilty of so many Rascalities in his public Character, that he is obliged to drink three bottles of Claret a day in order to acquire a stationary rubor and prevent him from the trouble of running backwards and forward for a blush once every five minutes. In the tropical Latitudes of this fellow's Nose I was obliged to fry.'

The Mortlock family were rewarded by public honours, the eldest son being knighted, the second son High Sheriff of Cambridge. John Mortlock's son Edmund was a fellow of Christ's and his son Frederick eloped with Sarah [FINCH], daughter of the iron merchant. Frederick's son John Frederick, born in 1809, was transported to Australia after threatening his uncle Edmund in his rooms in Christ's with a dagger and a pistol. His *Experiences of a Convict* has been edited by G. A. Wilkes and A. G. Mitchell, 1965. One of John Mortlock's former clerks, Samuel [FRANCIS], was Mayor in 1788, 1790, 1792 and 1794, but suffered later from Mortlock's opponents, being almost reduced to bankruptcy. He was alive in 1833.

[FISHER] Street may refer to George Fisher, Mayor in 1840, as well as to John Thomas and William Fisher, all bankers in the late eighteenth and early nineteenth centuries. George Fisher owned the brickworks, now Alexandra Gardens, close to the street of this name. Fisher's Lane may have a different origin. Another banking family were the FOSTERs: E. Foster was Mayor in 1836–7, Richard Foster (who bought BROOKLAND House in 1825) in 1839–40, C. F. Foster in 1847–8, again in 1854–5 and in 1860–2, and H. S. Foster in 1849–50, but no such obloquy attaches to them as did to the Mortlocks. The words 'Foster's Bank' are still visible on Lloyds Bank, facing Petty Cury. Later Mayors, included elsewhere in this book, include C. [HUMFREY], the architect (1837–8), C. FINCH, the iron-founder (1848–9), W. EKIN, the brewer (1855–6), P. BEALES, the coal and corn merchant (1856–7, 1866–7), S. HURRELL (1857–8, 1864–6), who took over Beales's business. W. B.

REDFERN (1883–7) founded an amateur dramatic club called the Bijou, about 1875. In 1896 he rebuilt St Andrew's Hall in St Andrew's Street as the New Theatre. In this he was strongly supported by John [WILLIS] Clark. The first production was of *Hamlet* by the Haymarket Theatre Company. The theatre continued till after the Second World War, when it was used as a music-hall and cinema, but was demolished and replaced by Janus House. Redfern made many sketches of Cambridge and the surrounding countryside. (See W. B. Redfern, *Old Cambridge. A Series of Original Sketches with Descriptive Letterpress*, 1876, reprinted 1974.) Horace DARWIN was Mayor in 1896–7 (see above, p. 76), and Joseph Ashworth STURTON followed in 1913–14. His father Joseph Sturton in 1879 bought the estate of Barnwell Abbey. Sturton Town Hall, Mill Road, built in 1881, was the Working Men's Liberal Club and Reading Room for many years. The Hall has also been a Salvation Army hall and a variety hall, and lastly the Kinema (now demolished), opened in 1917, which closed in the early 1970s. 'Sturton Town' is the area between East Road and the Mill Road railway bridge. J. A. Sturton himself owned a retail chemist's in Fitzwilliam Street and Thurston's bakery in St Andrew's Street. Sturton's Quinine and Iron Tonic 'enriches and purifies the Blood, strengthens the system, and imparts tone and energy to the Digestive Organs', said an advertisement of 1897. Sturton generously supported the Baptist Chapel in TENISON Road, and is said to have come from [SLEAFORD]. Sturton Brewery was founded in 1874 by William Warboys.

Another member of the Beales farmily was B. W. BEALES (1916–17). The brewer H. B. BAILEY was Mayor 1923–4.

Other Mayors were H. H. [HARRIS] (1852–3, 1863–4), A. G.

BRIMLEY (1853–4), A. I. TILLYARD (1899–1900), whose son E. M. W. Tillyard was Master of Jesus College and a writer on English literature of international reputation, and William [WARREN] (1850–1), a grocer whose shop was at 51 Bridge Street. (P. J. Warren was Mayor in 1964–5.) However, Warren Road is in a Trinity Hall cluster, and was named after a Fellow (1683–1745) of that college who was a minister of St Edward's Church.

James Henry Chesshyre DALTON (1903–4) graduated from Trinity. He was twelfth Wrangler in 1894, and MD in 1893. He published on smallpox vaccination and reform of the Poor Law, and was particularly concerned with Cambridge health, but did not practise as a doctor.

A. S. CAMPKIN (1904–5 and 1911–12) was a pharmacist at 11 Rose Crescent. An authority on canine species, he had many interests including botany and swimming. He was prominent in local photographic circles. Three Cambridge shops still have his name in their titles.

Sir Walter DURNFORD (1847–1926), Mayor in 1909, was Provost of King's, combining this with being Principal of the Cambridge University day training school for elementary teachers. In 1906 he produced Aeschylus' *Eumenides*, and thereby launched the poet Rupert Brooke on his Cambridge stage career. 'He was a man of great sweetness of character', wrote his successor as Provost, M. R. James, 'which he masked under a humorous incisiveness of manner.'

Edmund Courtenay PEARCE (1870–1935) after whom Pearce Close (not Pearce's Yard) is named, was first a school-master, then Vicar of St Bene't's, Master of Corpus Christi, and lastly Bishop of Derby. Mayor in 1917–18, and Chairman of Cambridgeshire County Council in 1927, 'few men', it was said of him, 'have given themselves with such unswerving loyalty to the service of society in School, College, University, Town, Country and Diocese'.

G. H. LAVENDER (1922–3) was a milliner and draper with premises at 9 Bene't Street, and on Peas Hill.

George Plume HAWKINS was Mayor in 1919–20 and 1921–2, and is remembered for his restaurant, the Dorothy Café ('the Dot') where young people met for *thés dansants*, as well as for another café in Cambridge. His catering business had been begun by his grandfather in 1838. During the First World War he catered for the Cambridgeshire Regiment. In 1903 he was a member of a committee dealing with an outbreak of smallpox, which brought him in daily contact with the disease until it was stamped out. No mean antiquary, he could speak about old Cambridge customs. He was a prominent Freemason. Three hundred employees attended his funeral in 1931.

E. JACKSON (1930–1) has as predecessor a namesake, Henry Jackson (1603).

Mrs Florence A. KEYNES (1932–3), the author of *By-ways of Cambridge History*, was one of the early students of Newnham College. She worked with the Cambridge Central Aid Society, and was for many years chairman of a committee in London of the National Council of Women. Her membership of the Borough Council began in 1914, when an Act of Parliament made it possible for married women to become candidates for seats on County and Borough Councils (only *un*married women had been allowed to do so). She was the mother of J. M. Keynes, the economist.

Sir Montagu [BUTLER] (1941–3) died in 1952 aged seventy-nine. He had been President of the Council of State, India, and Governor of the Isle of Man before being elected Master of

Pembroke (1937–48). A distinguished man of letters, he was the father of R. A. ('Rab') Butler, the Conservative politician, who was Master of Trinity from 1965. Henry Montagu Butler was master of Trinity 1886–1918.

George WILDING (1873–1956) was Mayor in 1944–5. He took a great interest in the Perse School for Boys, helped to found the Winston House Boys' Home and was chairman of the Cambridge branch of the United Nations Association. In 1945 he conferred the Honorary Freedom of the Borough on the 8th US Army Air Force.

Howard MALLETT (1954–5), 'a busy and jovial fellow', took a BA in theology from Fitzwilliam House and worked almost all his working life as an assistant in the University Library. He was also a Councillor for twenty years. His great interest in helping young people is shown by his appointment as Assistant County Commissioner for Cambridgeshire Boy Scouts, and his being awarded the Silver Acorn, the highest award of the Scouts. He was chairman of the local group for the Duke of Edinburgh Award and a governor of the Perse School. A Youth Club in STURTON Street was named after him.

Frank DOGGETT retired in 1967, aged seventy-nine, after forty years of unbroken membership of the City Council. He worked for the Cambridge Scientific Instrument Company as chief draughtsman of scientific instrument design, for fifty years (see Horace DARWIN), and was Mayor 1946–7. In retirement he still walked his dachshund three times a day.

Benjamin C. JOLLEY (1920–1) is remembered in Jolley Way, which is in a cluster of streets named after Mayors and other local people. B. A. Jolley, a prominent Wesleyan Methodist, lived in Meadowcroft, Chesterton, where a

Wesleyan Methodist Chapel was built in the garden in 1904. The chapel later became a Pye conference centre.

Later Mayors after whom streets have or may have been named are G. DEAN (1969–70), ROBERT MAY (1975–6), and R. E. [WRIGHT] (1976–7).

Churches and saints

The growth of population brought many new churches. ST BENE'T'S had existed since *c.* 1020, LITTLE ST MARY'S, Holy Sepulchre (the ROUND CHURCH) and ST BOTOLPH'S since the twelfth century, Great ST MARY'S since the twelfth century if not earlier, ST EDWARD'S and ST PETER'S since *c.* 1200, ALL SAINTS since the late thirteenth to the early fourteenth centuries (rebuilt in Jesus Lane 1864), and there were other medieval foundations not mentioned in street-names (viz., St Clement's, thirteenth century (there are gardens named after this), St Giles (fragments from the twelfth century), St Mary Magdalene (the 'Leper Chapel', twelfth century), St Michael (early fourteenth century), Holy Trinity (partly thirteenth century). No more were founded till the nineteenth century; then came CHRISTCHURCH (1837–9), ST PAUL'S (1841), ST ANDREW the Great (1842–3; on the site of a medieval church), the PRIORY or ABBEY Church (Little St Andrew's, early thirteenth century, restored *c.* 1854), ST MATTHEW'S (1866), ST BARNABAS (1870–88), ST LUKE'S (1874), ST MARK'S (1902–3, but an earlier church 1871), St John Evangelist (1896) and ST PHILIP'S (late nineteenth century) and others. These new foundations received large donations from colleges, and did much to create

communities in their areas. ST MARK'S received a large dona-
tion from a member of the University, Mr A. Vansittart, of
PINEHURST (at that time a single house, later being developed for blocks of flats).

Other saints' names, mentioned elsewhere, are ST
ANTHONY, ST BEDE, ST ELIGIUS, ST THOMAS. ST
CHRISTOPHER the legendary giant who carried the Christ-
child unawares, and ST STEPHEN, the first Christian martyr,
are named in contiguous streets. ST MARGARET'S is said to
be named after the wife of a builder. ST KILDA and ST
NEOTS are place-names. (St Kilda's Avenue has at the corner
with Campkin Road the 'Jenny Wren' pub. The island of St
Kilda's is known for its distinctive type of wren, *troglodytes,
troglodytes hirtensis.*) Sir St Vincent Cotton, a landowner, is
remembered in Cotton's Field and ST VINCENT'S Close. To
pay his debts, he sold by auction all his 725 acres in Girton
parish, north of Huntingdon Road. (St Vincent was the scene of
one of Nelson's victories.) ST TIBB is short for St Tibba, a relation of two daughters of Penda, King of Mercia, and patron
saint of falconers. The road used to lead to Falcon Yard, now
demolished. She was buried at Peterborough, says the *Anglo-
Saxon Chronicle* for 963 AD (See H. Thurston and D. Attwater,
eds., *Butler's Lives of the Saints* (4 vols., 1956).

The High Stewards: unprotected protectors

There were High Stewards of the University from 1418 or
earlier. The High Steward of the Borough was first elected in
1529. Each had the office of protecting the Borough or
University, preserving their privileges, trying certain offenders

against members of the University, safeguarding the rights of the Borough for its courts, even safeguarding each from the other. At the same time, and for a long period, they ran the risk of losing their lives. (See Keynes, *By-ways of Cambridge History*, p. 20 above.) In the nineteenth century the offices became honorary, and safe.

Two clusters, one near Arbury Road, the other off Newmarket Road, were named after many of these officers. Thomas HOWARD, Earl of Surrey and Duke of Norfolk (1473–1554) was elected for the Borough in 1529, when he was also High Steward for the University. He led the vanguard at the battle of Flodden, when the Scots were defeated, and later devastated the Scottish border. He incensed Henry VIII against WOLSEY, yet acquiesced in the execution of his own niece, Anne Boleyn. He was ousted from favour in 1547 by the Duke of SOMERSET, but survived in the Tower till the accession of Mary (1553), when he was restored to favour.

Edward [SEYMOUR], Earl of [HERTFORD], Duke of SOMERSET (1506?–52) (the first two names probably not intended), elected for the Borough in 1547, was Protector of his nephew, the boy Edward VI, and Chancellor of the University, where (and at Oxford) he seems to have been educated. He built the original Somerset House, by the Thames, 'too princely for a subject'. (However, Charles Seymour the sixth Duke of Somerset, Chancellor of the University 1689–1748, whose statue by Rysbrack stands in the Senate House, may also or alternatively have been intended.) The first duke's sister Jane was Henry VIII's third wife. His religious innovations, permitting free discussions, at length caused him to be unpopular, and he too was sent to the Tower, but though released he was condemned for a plot to rouse the country against 'the great' and to murder John DUDLEY, Duke of Warwick, for which he was beheaded on Tower Hill.

The same John Dudley, later Duke of NORTHUMBER-LAND (1502?–53) was elected for the Borough in 1552, and was Chancellor of the University. He married his son to [LADY JANE] Grey, whom he proclaimed Queen at the Cross in Cambridge Market, and thereby was in disfavour with Mary Tudor. Mary, before she was crowned, was even pursued to Sawston Hall but escaped. When she succeeded to the throne after the execution of Lady Jane, Dudley desperately rode to Cambridge, a turncoat to the last, and read the proclamation of Mary's succession, flinging his cap in the air at the market place to show his devotion to her and the Catholic cause, but in vain. He too went to the block, in 1553.

The grandson of Thomas HOWARD, also named Thomas, Duke of Norfolk (1536–72), elected for the Borough in 1554, fared no better. He contributed largely towards the completion of MAGDALENE College, but planned to marry Queen Elizabeth's rival, Mary, Queen of Scots, and was executed for high treason.

William, Baron [PAGET] (1505–63) was High Steward of the University, having been at Trinity Hall. (Paget Road and Close are not in either of the High Steward clusters.) He was one of Henry VIII's chief advisers, but, remaining faithful to Somerset, was arrested on a charge of conspiring against Warwick and degraded from the Order of the Garter. He sanctioned the proclamation of Queen Mary, and had her favour, but gave up his offices when Elizabeth succeeded. But Sir George Paget (1809–92), Regius Professor of Physic (Caius), or his brother Sir James may be remembered.

[NORTH] Street, parallel with Histon Road, is also not in either of the clusters, but could refer to the next High Steward of the Borough, the second Baron North, elected in 1572. ([NORTH] Terrace is probably named geographically.) He was MP for Cambridgeshire, Alderman of the Borough and Lord Lieutenant of the County, and was a great patron of actors and the theatre, which was lively in the University in the later years of Elizabeth's reign. He intervened with only partial success on behalf of two men accused of unlawful bear-baiting at Chesterton in 1581, who were jailed in Westminster. (See Alan H. Nelson, *Early Cambridge Theatres*, 1994.) It was his job to prepare Cambridgeshire for the coming of the Spanish Armada. With the harshness of his times, he condemned a student to stand in the pillory nailed to it by his ear. Also possible is Dr John North, Master of Trinity 1677–83, during whose Mastership much of the Wren Library was built.

Baron ELLESMERE (1540–1617) was also Viscount BRACKLEY. He was also named Thomas EGERTON. Elected High Steward of the Borough in 1600, he helped to determine the Act of Union between England and Scotland, and took part in the trial of Mary, Queen of Scots. He also petitioned the king to grant a charter to the Borough, giving it all the liberties of a free borough, for ever – but without prejudice to the University's interests, which nullified it.

A more famous name is that of Francis Bacon (1561–1626) (befriended by Ellesmere), remembered in VERULAM Way and ST ALBANS Road, since he was Viscount St Albans and signed himself with a name derived from the Roman name of that town, Verulamium. Elected as High Steward of the Borough in 1617, he had been MP for the University since 1614, but this did not save him from a brief imprisonment in the Tower. He entered Trinity College in 1573 and in 1605 published *The Advancement of Learning*, a review of the state of knowledge in his own time, and in 1620 his *Novum Organum*, in which he stressed the importance of experiment in interpreting Nature, insisting that contrary views of any thesis proposed must be considered. According to Aubrey's *Brief Lives*, not always dependable, he died after stuffing a hen with snow to preserve it. In his opposition to earlier ideas of authority, he became the practical creator of scientific induction. 'He made possible', wrote Christopher Hill, 'new attitudes towards history – progress without chiliasm, change without apocalypse, reformation without tarrying for the second coming.' His *Essays* are the most widely read of his works. There is a statue of him in Trinity College Chapel.

John [FINCH] (1584–1660), Baron Finch of FORDWICH, can also be remembered both for his family name and for his title, although 'Finch' appears separately from the cluster of High Steward names, and is also the name of a well-known family of ironmongers dating from 1688. (See above, p. 67.) Fordwich, being part of his title, and within the High Steward cluster, is best taken as referring to the baron. John Finch was elected High Steward in 1640, was Speaker of the House of Commons, but was impeached and fled to Holland. On his return to England at the Restoration he took part as Solicitor-General in the trial of the regicides, and as High Steward of the Borough presided at the trial of Stafford, the Catholic nobleman beheaded on the evidence of Titus Oates's perjuries.

While Baron Finch was abroad in 1652 Oliver CROMWELL took over the office of High Steward of the Borough.

[CLARENDON] Road, rather than the street of the same name, may well have been named after the High Steward of the Borough, Edward Hyde (1609–74), who was elected in 1660 and became Earl of Clarendon, but the road is not in either of the two High Steward clusters and is of earlier date than them. Hyde's connections are with Oxford, but he visited Cambridge as a young man, only to catch smallpox here. He was virtually head of the Government, while High Steward of Cambridge, and thus of great value on account of his influence, but like several of his predecessors in that office, fell victim to a court cabal, and in 1667 was impeached for high treason. He left for France, where he was nearly murdered by English seamen. His *History of the Rebellion in England*, published in 1704–7, remains now his great claim to fame. Perhaps, however, the younger brother of the Clarendon who served in [MELBOURNE's] government, Charles Pelham (1802–98) was intended. Like other Villiers Clarendons he was a Johnian. An MP for upwards of sixty years, he was a prominent opponent of the Corn Laws.

In 1688 Henry JERMYN (1636–1708) was elected for the Borough. Jermyn Street in London is also named after this courtier of Charles II, who followed James II in exile to France. He fought against William III at the Battle of the Boyne in Ireland, but was able to persuade the king to accept his apology, and retired to Cheveley. His title was Lord [DOVER], which is conceivably the origin of the name of the street off East Road, although it is not included in either of the two clusters of High Stewards' names. However, Joseph [YORKE] (1724–92) was also Baron Dover, and has Cambridgeshire connections, through the ownership of Wimpole Hall. A York House existed in living memory on Newmarket Road, at the other end of East Road from Dover Street.

William, Earl of CRAVEN (1606–97) was High Steward of the University 1667–97. His portrait wearing armour, by Gerrit Honthorst, is in the Fitzwilliam Musuem.

There are many Russells who have achieved fame. Edward [RUSSELL], Earl of Orford, was elected High Steward in 1698, although Russell Court and Street, off Hills Road, are not in either of the two clusters, and the origin of their names is uncertain. Later to be Duke of Bedford, Russell commanded the ship that brought William of Orange to England in 1688. He commanded the English and Dutch fleets that defeated the French at La Hogue, off Normandy, and so frustrated Louis XIV's intention of placing James II on the throne again. MP for Cambridgeshire and Lord Lieutenant of the County, he did not escape impeachment, but unlike many of his predecessors was acquitted.

The best known of the Russell family are Bertrand (1872–1970), the philosopher and anti-nuclear campaigner (but the street was named long before his time) and John, first Earl Russell (1792–1878), a leading figure in English politics. He proposed the Reform Bill of 1832 in the House of Commons and was Home Secretary in [MELBOURNE's] government in 1835. Prime Minister in 1846–52 and 1865, he held other great offices of state, was held to have mismanaged his Crimean policy, but did much for Italian unity. His brother Francis was High Steward in 1860.

Henry Bromley, first Baron MONTFORT, elected 1741, and his son Thomas, elected 1755, did nothing in politics comparable to what many of their predecessors had done. Henry inherited a large fortune, which he lost through lavish expenditure and gambling. He took his own life in 1755. Thomas also gambled heavily, and was obliged to sell his estate. He died in 1799. Unlike other High Stewards, the Montforts did not suffer on account of any national cause. (Simon de Montfort is not likely to have been intended.)

This was a time of great corruption in Cambridge. Among those who profited by the policy of selling 999 years' leases of land to Councillors were Samuel FRANCIS, James BURLEIGH, Peete MUSGRAVE, Thomas FRANCIS, and the heirs of Sir George DOWNING. Philip [YORKE], Earl of

[HARDWICKE] (1720–90), High Steward for the University, MP for Cambridgeshire, Lord Lieutenant of the County, dominated Cambridge politics in the 1770s and 1780s, becoming 'a lesser providence to whom all [Cambridge] matters must be reported. Any action taken without reference to him was a sort of treason', says the Victoria County History. He was, however, wise enough to see that the food riots caused by the war with France in 1756, by unemployment, heavy rain and speculative buying needed attention and ordered a weekly allowance of sixpence per head in several villages near his home in Wimpole. This did not prevent a riot in Cambridge on 15 June 1757, when 'a mob, chiefly of women' broke open a storehouse to take fifteen quarters of wheat. In 1795 there were riots again, quelled by the action of Mayor MORTLOCK, who sold publicly meat that the attackers supposed had been unlawfully kept back. But in comparison with the rest of East Anglia, Cambridge was quiet during this period. (See Paul Muskett, *'Riotous Assemblies'. Popular Disturbances in East Anglia 1740–1822*, EARO, The Resource Centre, Back Hill, Ely, 1984.)

The borough was no better off in the time of John Henry [MANNERS], Duke of RUTLAND, elected in 1800 as High Steward. He worked hand-in-glove with John MORTLOCK, making the Cambridge constituency a pocket borough in which voters were openly bribed. He was attacked by Hatfield, editor of the *Cambridge Independent Press*, and by George Pryme, a former Fellow of Trinity, as well as by satires like 'The Ratland Feast', attacking the freemen who

> . . . for a glass of wine
> Cringed at the Eagle once a month to dine.

Other opponents protested at 'the secret and unconstitutional influence of a noble family', but could not prevail at a time when non-resident voters could be brought in to vote 'just as gentlemen take a pack of hounds to cover'. Cambridge remained in the Rutland pocket till the Reform Bill of 1832. The Duke was removed from office in 1836. The family name is not remembered in a street-name unless MANERS Way, near Queen Edith's Way, is a mis-spelling – Manners does appear on one popular map of recent times.

[WENTWORTH] Road is not in one of the clusters, but might be supposed to be named after Charles William Wentworth, Earl FITZWILLIAM (1786–1857), elected High Steward for the Borough in 1850, who supported Parliamentary reform and free trade. (However, Mary Wentworth was allocated land in the Chesterton Inclosure, and is more likely to have been intended.) FITZWILLIAM Road could also recall the Earl, but the Street, opposite the Fitzwilliam Museum, is clearly named after the founder of the museum, Richard seventh Viscount Fitzwilliam of Meryon (1745–1816) (who has no connection with the Earl).

From this time onwards the title is honorific. Lord Macaulay, the historian and poet, was elected High Steward of the Borough in 1857, but neither he nor the High Steward Francis Osborne, Lord Godolphin, elected 1836, has a street named after him, although a Macaulay Avenue is shown on a post-1945 Barnett map, between Mortlock Avenue and Maitland Avenue.

William [CAVENDISH] (1808–91), seventh Duke of Devonshire, who was High Steward of the Borough, Chancellor of the University, and founder at great personal expense of the Cavendish Laboratory, where some of the most significant discoveries in science have been made, may be remembered in [DEVONSHIRE] Road. However, the eighth

Duke, Spencer Compton Cavendish (1833–1908), his eldest son, was also at Trinity, was awarded an honorary doctorate of law, was a Liberal MP, Chancellor of the University and very prominent in politics, declining the premiership three times. He formed the Liberal Unionist party, and held high offices under Gladstone, whom he opposed over Home Rule for Ireland. He was not a High Steward.

Colonel Thomas [HARDING]'s surname appears not in a cluster of High Stewards, but in a cluster of military names. Elected High Steward in 1907, and born at Madingley Hall (now the property of the University), he was an engineer, who had been Lord Mayor of Leeds and was High Sheriff of the counties of Cambridgeshire and Huntingdonshire in 1900. He owned 1,700 acres of land in the county.

Alternatively, Sir John Harding, first Baron Petherton, born in 1896, British field-marshal, may have been commemorated. HARDING Way is close to TEDDER Way, DOWDING Way and HARRIS Road, all named after high-ranking RAF officers of the Second World War. Sir John was chief of staff of the Allied Army in Italy in 1944, later governor-general of Cyprus at the time when Archbishop Makarios opposed the British, and organised the combat against terrorism there. He was created baron in 1958.

Victor Christian Cavendish, ninth Duke of Devonshire, was elected High Steward of the Borough in 1929, and was High Steward also of the University. He is not likely to have been named personally in the relevant streets, which were named before his time, nor is George Douglas Newton, Baron ELTISLEY of Croxton, also High Steward for the Borough and MP, for the same reason.

John Maynard KEYNES (1883–1946), Baron Keynes of

Tilton, elected for the Borough in 1943, is named in the cluster off Newmarket Road. He was the pioneer of the theory of full employment, especially in *A Treatise of Money* (1930) and the *General Theory of Employment, Interest and Money* (1936), arguing that unemployment, prevalent in his time, was not incurable. He influenced Roosevelt's 'New Deal' administration, and is still cited today in economic arguments. An undergraduate and Fellow of King's College, for which, as Bursar, he made a fortune, and a member of the 'Bloomsbury' group including Leonard and Virginia Woolf and E. M. Forster, he married Lydia Lopokova, a ballerina, and financed the building of the Arts Theatre in Cambridge. It was said of him that 'he understood better than most the supreme importance of Aristotle's dictum that the proper aim of business is the provision of leisure'. He accepted the Order of Merit just before his death. (See Florence Keynes, *Gathering Up the Threads*, 1950.)

Inclosures

Under the General Inclosures Acts of 1801, 1836 and 1845 the many, uneconomically divided, strips of land dating often from medieval times were allocated to local people. This improved the technical efficiency of farming in the Agricultural Revolution, which had begun in the eighteenth century and earlier. (See ORWELL FURLONG, p. 15.) Allocations are recorded in the Barnwell area (1811) to Thomas PANTON, the Reverend John C. BULLEN (who owned large areas near to the present Bullen Close), James BURLEIGH, Charles [HUMFREY], John LENS, Peete MUSGRAVE, John [PYKE] and F. C. J. PEMBERTON; in Cherry Hinton (1806) to Mary VENTRIS, John [PYKE], Robert RICKARD and Samuel SALMONS (near Salmon Lane); in Chesterton (extending to Huntingdon Road) to William Henry APTHORPE, John ATKINS, Thomas ATKINS, Ann BEALES, Mary BENSON (in the area of Benson street), Richard FOSTER, Rt Hon. Charles Philip, Earl of HARDWICKE, John HAVILAND and to several of the GREEN family (cf. Green's Road), while Clare Hall (now Clare College) received Great FRANK'S Lane. Other recipients of land in Chesterton were Jeremiah KENT, John LARKIN and widow LARKIN, William LIVERMORE, Thomas MARKHAM, Charles THRIFT, Charles WAGSTAFF (including FRANK'S Lane), Mary WENT-WORTH, Elizabeth WILES, John Thomas WOODHOUSE, Mary Wragg and William Wragg (cf. Mrs Wragg GURNEY, under 'Benefactors', p. 134). Almost all of these names occur in streets in the area of their allocation (except PANTON, MUS-GRAVE, [PYKE], PEMBERTON, [HARDWICKE], whose names are remembered in other parts of Cambridge).

In Cherry Hinton LEETE Close is allocated to the Vicar; MALLETS and NUTTINGS occur as field-names there. Thomas MARKHAM is also shown as holding land in St Clement's parish, as is Richard WHEELER. DAWS Lane is allocated to John Headley.

In Trumpington (1819) a receipt is signed by John MARIS, churchwarden, and allocations are recorded to the Reverend Christopher ANSTEY and Francis Charles James PEMBER-TON.

DRAYTON Close and KEATES Close are recorded as names from an old Inclosure in Cherry Hinton. SHEPHERD'S Close (Cherry Hinton) was the subject of an award dated 18

Free School Lane

December 1810, made to Gonville and Caius College. [PEN], in a street parallel to Shepherd's Close, may refer to a sheep-pen.

The twentieth century

THE LATER COLLEGES

Like her ancestor Victoria, Queen ELIZABETH II is celebrated in a road and a bridge opened in 1971. Her grandson PRINCE WILLIAM is also remembered. (Victoria bridge was opened in 1895.) In late Victorian times the University began to expand more than it had ever done. The first colleges, still surviving, that were founded then were for women, although Cavendish College was founded, almost opposite CAVENDISH Avenue, in 1876, to provide facilities for taking University courses and obtaining degrees at moderate cost. (SELWYN was founded for the same purpose.) It also provided training for intending schoolmasters, but closed in 1891. HOMERTON College, London, which was founded in 1659 to aid Congregational churches, then took over the site from 1894 as a teachers' training college, but was adopted by the University in 1977. FITZWILLIAM House was initiated in 1869, in a house bearing the date 1727 opposite the Fitzwilliam Museum, and had facilities like those of Cavendish College, but became a recognised college of the University in 1966. Hughes Hall, founded in 1896 (as the Cambridge Training College for Women from 1885), was named after Elizabeth Philips Hughes. St Edmunds' House took a broadly similar course to that of Fitzwilliam House, but the last two have no street named after them, nor have Lucy Cavendish (1965) and Wolfson (1973, as University College from 1965) Colleges.

NEWNHAM College, still today exclusively for women, had a house at 74 Regent Street in 1871, and built its first building in 1875. GIRTON College started at Hitchin in 1869, and moved to its present site in 1873. It was exclusively for women until 1979, when men were also admitted. Professor Henry SIDG-WICK (1838–1900), a Trinity philosopher and agnostic, was prominent in advocating the admission of the women to the University. Clare Hall, a graduate college, was founded in 1966; DARWIN, also for graduates, was created in 1964. Churchill College (1958) and New Hall (1954) have no streets named after them.

ROBINSON College (1977) was named after its founder, Sir David Robinson (1904–87), who made a fortune in the radio and television rental business, and later in horse-racing. 'A self-effacing philanthropist, he gave all his money away', to the college and many other beneficiaries.

SCIENTISTS

Of the many Nobel prizewinners for science three have streets named after them. Lord ADRIAN (1889–1977) was a laureate in 1932 for work on the function of neurons – the street leads, suitably, to Addenbrooke's Hospital (but is shown without a name on the Heffers map of 1995). Lord Adrian was Master of Trinity, Professor of Physiology at Cambridge and President of the Royal Society. Lady Adrian was prominent in caring for mental welfare. The Lady Adrian School opened on COURT-NEY Way in 1956. Both husband and wife may be remembered here.

Ernest RUTHERFORD, Baron Rutherford of Nelson and Cambridge (1871–1937), was born in Nelson, New Zealand, where he graduated. He then went to work under Sir J. J. Thomson, as a member of Trinity. His first independent work was done at Montreal and Manchester. His influence on scientific thought has been compared with that of Faraday and Newton: he developed the nuclear theory of atomic structure, and was awarded the Nobel Prize for Chemistry in 1908. In 1919, when he became Cavendish Professor of Experimental Physics at Cambridge, he published the first evidence for the transmutation of matter, explaining the phenomenon as a subatomic chemical change in which one element spontaneously transmutes into another. He inspired many spectacular discoveries after 1933, leading to the creation of atomic energy and the atom bomb. (See Egon Larsen, *The Cavendish Laboratory*, 1962.)

ALEX WOOD (b. 1879), Fellow of Emmanuel, assisted Rutherford, and published on *The Physical Basis of Music*, as well as a *Life of Thomas Young*, discoverer of the wave-theory of light and the almost successful decipherer of the Rosetta Stone. Wood was prominent in the Peace Pledge Union, and Labour Candidate for Parliament. The Cambridge Labour Party HQ in NORFOLK Street is named after him.

Sir John Douglas COCKCROFT (1897–1967), sizar of St John's, developed with E. T. S. Walton the high-voltage particle-accelerator machine that bears their name. He persuaded RUTHERFORD that the Cavendish Laboratory should have a cyclotron. He took over the Mond Laboratory from Kapitza, the Russian scientist, who celebrated Rutherford with a crocodile on the wall of that building. Major advances in radar, but for which the Battle of Britain might have been lost, were due to Cockcroft. He began atomic energy research at Harwell, having a vision of cheap nuclear power. First Master of Churchill College, he was nominated by Churchill himself. He received the OM in 1957, the Nobel Prize for physics (with E. T. S. Walton) in 1951 and the Atoms for Peace award in 1961. Deeply interested in architecture and music, 'he was a man of few words, and his writing was minute'.

Sir German Sims [WOODHEAD] was a Fellow of Trinity Hall and Professor of Pathology 1899–1921. He helped to found the settlement for tubercular patients at Papworth. However, Mayor Woodhead is at least as likely to have been intended.

Sir Frederick Gowland HOPKINS (1861–1947), 'the father of British biochemistry', was appointed Professor of that subject in 1914, and when the Sir William Dunn Institute, near the street named after him, was founded in 1921 he was given the new chair founded with it. He was awarded the Nobel Prize in 1929, for his work on vitamins. A pupil of his at Emmanuel, from where he went on to Trinity, wrote 'He had faith that the chemical processes underlying life itself were ultimately explicable and accessible to research. His humility was remarkable for its absolute sincerity.' MOORE is the name of his deputy at the Dunn Institute.

MUSICAL COMPOSERS

STERNDALE Close is named after Sterndale Burrows, Coroner in the 1970s and 1980s, who owned the land. An ancestor was Sir William Sterndale Bennett (1816–75), who, brought up an orphan, was a King's chorister, and became Professor of Music in Cambridge in 1856, principal of the Royal Academy of Music in 1866. He was highly regarded by Mendelssohn and Schumann for his many symphonies, concertos, songs and piano pieces. Two musical composers of this century have given their names to streets. Benjamin BRITTEN (Baron Britten)

(1913–76) conducted his arrangement of Gay's *The Beggar's Opera* in Cambridge in 1948 and thereafter often visited Cambridge. Among his best-known works are the operas, *Peter Grimes*, *Albert Herring*, *Let's Make an Opera*, *Billy Budd*, also *War Requiem*, *Serenade* for tenor, horn and strings and the Third String Quartet. Sir Arthur BLISS (1891–1975) studied at Pembroke, and made music with Cambridge University Music Society. He became Music Director of the BBC and Master of the Queen's Music. His best-remembered works are the music for ballets, *Checkmate* and *Miracle in the Gorbals*, and his film music for *The Shape of Things to Come*. Both composers received Honorary Degrees from the University in 1964. (See Frida Knight, *Cambridge Music*, 1980.)

THE ARMED SERVICES

Military men are remembered in two clusters in north Cambridge. Best known is Bernard Law MONTGOMERY (1887–1976), first Viscount Montgomery of Alamein, where he launched the battle in 1942 which turned the tide against the Germans in North Africa. He was commander of the ground forces for the invasion of Normandy in 1944, and accepted the German surrender on Lüneburg Heath. Churchill said of him he was 'in defeat unbeatable; in victory unbearable'. He became Field Marshal in 1944. Parallel with Montgomery Road, WAVELL Way is named after Archibald Percival Wavell (1883–1950), first Earl Wavell, Field Marshal, who was in 1939 given the Middle East Command. He defeated an Italian army in North Africa, capturing 150,000 prisoners, and conquered Abyssinia from the Italians. After that his military fortune declined, though Rommel admired him. He was Viceroy of

India 1943–7, and published, unusually for a military man, an anthology of verses, *Other Men's Flowers*. Between WAVELL and MONTGOMERY comes Andrew Browne CUNNING-HAM, Viscount Cunningham of Hyndhope (1883–1963), admiral of the fleet. In the First World War he took part in the raid on Zeebrugge; in the Second he gained a major victory over the Italian fleet off Cape Matapan. In 1942 he was appointed Allied Naval Commander, Expeditionary Force under Eisenhower, covering the invasion of Sicily and the Salerno landings. He received honorary degrees from many universities, including Cambridge, and is commemorated close to the Nelson monument in Trafalgar Square. He would truckle to nobody, not even Churchill, when required to take action he considered unsound. In another cluster, nearby, Marshal of the RAF, Arthur William TEDDER, later First Baron Tedder of Glenguin (1890–1967), who assisted Montgomery in North Africa by his attacks on Italy, and later, as Eisenhower's deputy, by preventing German forces from reaching the Normandy beachhead, is also commemorated. He was Chancellor of the University in 1950, after the candidature of Jawaharlal Nehru was withdrawn. Also nearby is the street named after Hugh Caswall Tremenheere DOWDING, First Baron Dowding (1882–1970), who was Air Chief Marshal, and as Commander-in-Chief of Fighter Command was in charge during the Battle of Britain when the Luftwaffe was shattered. Deeply moved by the deaths of so many fighter pilots, he wrote books on spiritualism and theosophy. Also in the same cluster is the name of Sir Arthur Travers HARRIS (b. 1892), known as 'Bomber' Harris for his policy, as Commander-in-Chief of Bomber Command, of mass bombing-raids on German cities. (H. H. Harris was Mayor in 1852–3 and 1863–74 but is less likely to have been intended, in view of the closeness of other RAF names, but that is no reason for not remembering him too.) In a Peterhouse cluster occurs the name of William Riddell BIRDWOOD (1865–1951), Field Marshal. He was in command of the Anzac Corps in the Gallipoli landing of 1915 and in France till 1918. In 1925 he was Commander-in-Chief of the Indian army. From 1930 to 1938 he was Master of Peterhouse.

POLITICIANS

The second Marquess of ZETLAND (1876–1961), Lawrence John Lumley Dundas, graduate of Trinity, was Conservative MP for Hornsey 1907–16, and played a great part in the administration of India, of which he was Secretary of State, until 1940, when disagreement with Churchill made it impossible for him to continue. He was deeply impressed by Indian philosophy, one of his many works on India being translated into Sanskrit. In 1935 appeared his *Steps to Indian Home Rule*. He received an honorary LL D from Cambridge and from Glasgow, as well as an honorary LittD from Leicester University.

The name [TENBY] could refer to Viscount Tenby, Gwilym Lloyd George (1894–1967), second son of David Lloyd George, and Liberal MP, who was a graduate of Jesus and successively in wartime Minister of Fuel and Power, Minister of Food and Home Secretary.

William Wedgwood Benn, First Viscount [STANSGATE] (1877–1960) was a Liberal MP 1906–27, when he joined the Labour Party. He was Secretary for India and Secretary for Air. His son Tony Wedgwood Benn (b. 1925) renounced his title and was thus able to continue as a member of the House of Commons. The son held several ministerial posts in Labour

Governments, always standing for left-wing Labour views. The name Stansgate is unusual, which lends some likelihood to the attribution here. [WEDGEWOOD] Drive in Cherry Hinton may also be related, if mis-spelt.

RACKHAM Close can only refer to Clara Dorothea Tabor, MA, JP, Borough Councillor, Fellow and Associate of Newnham College, who in 1901 married H. Rackham, Senior Tutor of Christ's. She was a suffragette and a tireless promoter of good causes. She died in 1966, aged ninety.

LANDOWNERS, FARMERS AND BUSINESSMEN

Landowners can be as influential as builders, when street-names are decided. William (Bill) FISON owned a thirty-seven-acre field which he sold in 1972 to a developer who sold it to the Council. (The forenames in neighbouring streets are not those of his children.) Dr John Lens (1756–1825), Sergeant-at-Law, later King's Serjeant (formerly the highest rank of barrister), who took his BA at St John's and became a law Fellow of Downing, owned the land on which LENSFIELD Road was built. His independence became proverbial, giving rise to the toast, 'Serjeant Lens and the independence of the bar'.

An ancestor of the family of Francis, of Quy Hall, who owned land in Fen Ditton, was Thomas MUSGRAVE FRANCIS (1850–1931), son of Clement Francis. A photograph of him appears in C. Jackson, *A Cambridge Bicentenary*, 1990, where he is called Lord of the Manor and owner of Quy Hall. He did public service as a magistrate, visitor to prisons and in many other ways. An old Etonian, he was thought of as 'a very great gentleman': 'there was an air about him of courtlier days but he could be stern when occasion arose'. His father Clement

Francis was involved in legal work connected with the reconciliation of the University and the Borough in the mid-nineteenth century, as well as the coprolite boom (see DE FREVILLE, p. 65), railway development and the case of John Frederick MORTLOCK.

A GLEBE is a plot of land owned by a church, usually providing part of the incumbent's stipend. Glebe Road was such a plot, as is ST ANDREW'S GLEBE. BISHOP'S Road and Court were originally on glebe land.

Similarly farmers are remembered in the places where their farms were, like William DOWNHAM, who occupied Manor Farm, hence Manor Community College. The road was named in 1982. The reminiscences of a member of the Downham family are recorded by Sallie Purkis (see p. 1 above.) (However, MANOR Street, far from the college, marks the boundary of the old Manor Gardens in Jesus Lane. The Manor House that stood on the site of All Saints vicarage was demolished in 1831.) Henry WETENHALL owned hopfields and lived in Maids' Causeway in the middle of the nineteenth century. His offices were in St Andrew's Hill. Edward WRIGHT, a farmer, was chairman of Fen Ditton parish council for forty years. His son Charles died in 1996. The family has farmed in Fen Ditton since 1880, and the son Edward Wright still does so in 1999.

VENTRESS Close and Ventress Farm Court bear the names of the owners of a farm who appear in the *Cambridge Chronicle* between 1801 and 1832. W. Ventriss advertised there on 6 December 1816 that he would prosecute undergraduates for riding over the lands and breaking down the fences in the parish of Cherry Hinton. Thomas Ventris was Mayor in 1559. Tony Ventres (d. 1978) was well known on Cambridge Market.

HALL FARM was in the area round Hall Farm Road. WHITEHILL Road records where White Hill Farm was – the original name in *c.* 1824 was White Hall; as usual in Cambridge, hills appear where others might see only flat land. NEWNHAM CROFT (croft = farm) gave its name to the present street. [OWLSTONE] Croft is the name of a house that gave its name to the street, of which the surname Oulston or the village of the same name in Yorkshire is probably the origin. SCOT-LAND Farm stood in the area where there are now many other names referring to Scotland: EDINBURGH, INVERNESS, KINROSS, STIRLING, DUNDEE. (ENNISKILLEN in the same area is in Ireland.) Not in this area but also Scottish are BURNSIDE, MONTROSE, ROXBURGH, PENTLANDS, ST KILDA.

COWLEY Road, being across the railway tracks from NUFFIELD Road, must have been named after Lord Nuffield's motor-car works at Cowley, Oxford. There is no obvious Cambridge connection.

A mill, still standing, by the Mill House in French's Road, and built about 1848, was owned by William FRENCH. It was known as New Chesterton Mill. The sails were removed in 1912, and it was not used at all after 1956, when Edwin French died. (The name of the road till *c.* 1892 was OCCUPATION Road, but it was known locally by the name of the mill-owners. An 'occupation road' is a private road for the use of occupiers of the land. The road off Newmarket Road that still goes by this name has retained it after it was no longer appropriate.)

The name Nutters in NUTTERS Close occurs in the name of an island near Sheep's Green, but is also in memory of the Nutter family who owned the mill at Grantchester, and the King's Mill at the end of Mill Lane, and the mill in Long Road.

Shop owners are remembered in HEATH House, named after George Heath, Director of Eaden LILLEY'S department store, who died in 1956. A prominent member of Emmanuel Congregational Church, he was a founder-member of the Cam Sailing Club, and had rowed for YMCA Boat Club. Kenneth Eaden Lilley was chairman of the management committee of the Hundred Houses Society, which built FALLOWFIELD. The street named after him is in the same area.

NURSERY Walk appears to be in the area of the Cumbrian Nurseries, which were in business in the 1920s.

GREEN'S Road is named after Arthur William Green, a carpenter and builder, with premises (Barker and Green) there in 1887.

Thomas P. N. [CHALK] died in 1960, aged seventy-six. He had been senior partner in a firm of auctioneers, surveyors and valuers, and lived at Rectory Farm, Cherry Hinton, not far from Chalk Grove (which is, however, near chalk pits). He was one of the original members of the Cambridge Amateur Boxing Club.

The origin of [MARSHALL] Road is obscure. It is too old to have been named after the economist Alfred Marshall (1842–1924) – 'it's all in Marshall', as many generations of undergraduates were taught – and there are several possible candidates. (See BLINCO, p. 89.) The founder of Marshall's AIRPORT, however, is remembered in that name and in THE MARSHALL WAY. Sir Arthur Marshall was knighted in 1974 for services to the RAF. The airport named after him had grown from 1927 into a works that designed and built the droop nose for Concorde and a rocket for positioning satellites. In 1929 a flying school opened. 20,000 airmen were trained here in the Second World War, after which a runway long enough to allow the largest aircraft to land for repairs was built. The Marshall Group now conducts business also in machine manufacture, aircraft design, bus construction, military engineering, car sales and services, and takes particular interest in the community, especially the local Air Training Corps Squadron. Sir Arthur, a graduate and honorary Fellow of Jesus, was a keen pilot, and an athlete of Olympic standard.

BANHAM'S Close relates to Banham's marina, further downstream from the street so named, shown as 'Dock' on the 1955 OS map. It closed c. 1970. It was from such a dock, where H. C. Banham began boat-building in 1906, that the hired boats set out on boat racing days in summer, rowed by undergraduates taking parents and girlfriends to moor by the banks, and cheer on the crews, between eating fruitcake and cucumber sandwiches. Earlier the Dant family operated from here a steam tug and the CUTTER FERRY, superseded by a footbridge in 1927. (See R. Cory, *Fenland Lighters and Horse Knockers*, EARO, The Resource Centre, Back Hill, Ely, 1977.)

Robert [FELTON] had an oil, lamp, colour and paper-hanging warehouse at 28 Mill Road. The street is said locally to be named after him, although a Master of Pembroke, Nicholas Felton (1556–1626), had the same surname. (There are no 'Pembroke' names in this area.)

SWANN'S Road was opened on 21 November 1987 to serve the MERCERS' Row Industrial Estate. This must be in memory of Swann's brickyard, 'near Stourbridge Common', mentioned in Council Minutes of 1903, which was in the same area. Swann's Terrace may also be connected, but it is off Mill Road, nowhere near the Industrial Estate. It is referred to in Council Minutes of 1904. (Cf. Swann HURRELL, pp. 66–7.) 'Mercers' must refer to booths at STOURBRIDGE Fair.

DESMOND Avenue is named after Desmond January, estate agent and son of the estate agent D. L. January, whose initials appear in the names of the three office-blocks on the south side of STATION Road: Demeter, Leda, Jupiter. Daedalus came later.

The OS map of 1885, revised 1925, shows a steam-plough works near PAMPLIN Court. (The first steam-plough was worked in the Netherlands in 1862.) This works was owned by a member of the Pamplin family, well known in Cherry Hinton.

Thomas KINGSTON, who owned houses in SLEAFORD Street, died in 1902 at the age of ninety-six. He had studied medicine briefly at King's College London, but made a fortune out of a clever investment, and hoarded his money. Known locally as 'Miser Kingston', even as a boy, according to his obituary, he watered farm workers' ale to make it go further. His clothing was shabby. He preferred slippers to boots, and when he wore boots never, for some unfathomable reason, wore two of a pair. Saving every farthing, he gave money to some poor widows, and bequeathed £100,000 – some millions in 1990s currency – to the Evangelical Party in the Church of England, or so the same obituary states. He also had built in 1877, and furnished entirely at his own expense, a wooden church called ST PHILIP'S, the predecessor of the present church, connected with St Barnabas Church. He directed that his coffin be made not of oak but of ash, and it was.

A Baron [GREYSTOKE] is said to have owned land in Cherrry Hinton.

The Cambridge banker Ebenezer FOSTER (d. 1851) bought the estate of ANSTEY Hall in 1838. It remained in the Foster family till it was sold to a tenant, who in 1950 resold it to the Ministry of Agriculture for the Plant Breeding Institute.

ROSEFORD Road, as a Mr Taylor remembers, was the name given by him, referring to Rose Fordham, the builder's niece. (See Purkis, *Arbury Is Where We Live.*) It was begun in 1936, but the outbreak of war stopped building.

[BRITANNIC] Way, in an industrial plot, suggests perhaps a name given by a patriotic exporter.

CLERGY

The rector of Fen Ditton, who retired in 1956, is commemorated in STANBURY Close. He served the parish throughout the Second World War, when he was ARP Warden.

LEETE Road is named after a Vicar of St Andrew's, Cherry Hinton.

A home for retired clergy was opened by Lord Fairhaven in [ALLEN] Court.

BENEFACTORS

COURTNEY Way is named after Lord Courtney (1832–1918), a benefactor of St John's. A Liberal MP, he was an enthusiast for proportional representation, and strongly opposed the Boer War and the First World War, always arguing for conciliation.

Mr M. F. A. FRASER was a benefactor of Trinity Hall in about 1930 (CHESTERFIELD and WARREN of the same college are in the same cluster), who was at one time a British Consul in China.

Mrs Wragg GURNEY, who died in 1921, left 403 acres to St John's, of which college her husband had been a Fellow. The college sold much of the land for building in 1930, the rest after

1945. 'As rich as the Gurneys' is a saying used in Gilbert and Sullivan's *Trial by Jury*, referring to a Norwich family.

Mrs Mary [RAMSDEN] (d. 1745) had considerable wealth, out of which she paid for a great increase in the Fellowship of St Catharine's, and for the Ramsden Building in that college. Ramsden Square is near to land allocated to the college under the Inclosure Acts, but mention may be made of Dr Ramsden, Vicar of St Andrew's Chesterton in 1814 and Professor of Divinity, who chaired a meeting in February 1808 to discuss the possibility of a non-sectarian school in Cambridge.

WORTS' CAUSEWAY was made from a benefaction by William Worts (d. 1709) of £1,500, for a causeway to run from Emmanuel College to the Gogs.

OTHERS

[ALPHA] Terrace, it has been suggested (by Shirley Brown, *Trumpington in Old Picture Postcards*, Zaltbommel, Netherlands, 1986, no. 49), may have been so called because it was the first road that set out to be a residential road. It was at one time called Scott's Row, Scott being the builder of many of the houses. [ALPHA] Road, built at about the same time in Chesterton, may have been named for the same reason.

[ALWYNE] is a family name of the Marquess of Northampton.

[BACHELORS'] Walk by the river in the grounds of St John's is mentioned in 1780. It could have been reserved for Bachelors.

BALDOCK Way is named after Edward Baldock, for many years verger of the nearby church of St John the Evangelist. One of the carved heads in the clerestory windows is of him. His ancestors presumably came from Baldock, originally so named after Baghdad, called Baldak by Mandeville. The name was given by Knights Templar who held the manor.

BENIANS Court is named after the historian and Master of St John's, 1933–52, Ernest Alfred Benians, who was born in 1880 and died in 1952, after a lifetime of service to the college.

There is an article on BROAD Street in the *Cambridge Evening News* for 7 March 1963, with a photograph said to contrast with the impression given by the name.

John BUCHAN, Baron Tweedsmuir (1875–1940), a Scotsman, the author of *The Thirty Nine Steps*, *Montrose*, *Prester John* and other famous novels, is remembered in a cluster of Scottish names: CALEDON, JEDBURGH, MONTCREIFF, possibly also [CAMERON], near the cluster. He was a Governor-General of Canada. There is a BANFF and a CALLANDER in Canada as well as in Scotland.

CAVESSON (a nose-band for troublesome horses), MARTINGALE (a strap passing between a horse's forelegs), and PELHAM (a bit, combining a snaffle and a curb in one) are all in one cluster of names in north Cambridge. There was formerly a paddock here.

CHURCH RATE Walk: a 'church-rate' is 'an assessment for the sustentation of the fabric, etc., of the parish church.' It is near LAMMAS Field, and 'Lammas rate' was a name also used for 'parish rate'.

BURNT CLOSE is shown as a field-name on a map of Grantchester in 1666.

CROME DITCH and STULP FIELD are also ancient field-names, as are probably Tabrum (Latin for 'pestilence') and Sladwell (not on the Heffers/OS map of 1995) in Grantchester. Widnall Close, also in Grantchester (not on the Heffers/OS map either), is named after Samuel Page Widnall, who lived in the Old Vicarage. His father Samuel Widnall was a famous dahlia grower with a nursery in the same village. (See E. N. Willmer, *Old Grantchester*, 1976.)

The Trumpington village cross was put up by John Stokton (d. *c.* 1475) at CROSS Hill. The base is preserved in the church. There is now a War Memorial cross carved by Eric Gill, erected in 1921.

DENNIS WILSON was President of the Cambridgeshire Branch of the British Legion. It was for services to the Legion that the street, opened by the Duchess of Kent, was named after him in 1981.

EASTFIELD, the name of an area of Chesterton as well as of a street, was built by the Hundred Houses Association in the 1930s, adding *c.* 1955–6 the SCOTLAND Road Estate. FALLOWFIELD was also developed in the 1930s.

EDENDALE Close is in the grounds of Edendale House.

GAZELEY Lane is named after the village near Newmarket; the Rector was the father of Mrs Wright, the first occupant of Gazeley House. The name 'Goldeslie' on a brick pillar presents a poser.

GEORGE PATEMAN was Assistant Secretary to the Board of Extramural Studies at Mill Lane.

GREEN PARK was suggested by Mr C. N. Naylor and accepted by the City Council on 3 February 1935. It leads out of Green End Road.

[THE HOMING], close to the aerodrome, suggests a navigational method, 'homing in'. [THE WESTERING] ('that which moves in a westerly direction') has a similar hint of navigating aircraft.

HURST House is shown on Bacon's map of *c.* 1908 in the area of the present Hurst Park Avenue. The flats named Dalegarth now occupy its site.

KATHLEEN ELLIOTT was Secretary of Cambridge Housing Society for nineteen years.

LAUNDRESS Lane leads to Laundress Green, beyond the old mill race, a drying-ground for University laundresses and local washerwomen. The Green was 'gay with washing fluttering and dancing in the breeze', Margaret Keynes, in *A House by the River*, remembered. Carpets and mats were brought out for beating too, until vacuum-cleaners were introduced.

[LONG] Road was once Mill Road, because of the mill at the Trumpington end, where the Old Mill House still stands. The newer name must refer to its unusual length.

[MOUNT PLEASANT], as in many cities, could well be named after the London street. DOWNING Street was named after the founder of the college, who gave his name also to Downing Street in London. HYDE PARK CORNER and COVENT GARDEN (where there was once an orchard) also have London names.

PEARCE'S Yard (not Close) is named after the Pearce family who lived in Grantchester 1890–1939. D. F. Pearce was a graduate of Trinity. There is a plaque in Grantchester Church in memory of the Pearces.

NORTHAMPTON was in 1796 (when the street was still named Bell Lane, after the 'Bell' inn) the end of a day's journey by Smith and Co.'s post coach, where passengers could stay overnight before going on to Birmingham (£1.11s.6d all the way).

William Phene NEALE was resident in Cherry Hinton Hall in 1904, and was at that time Lord Mayor of London.

RIVERSIDE is the Haling (i.e. towing) Way on Bacon's map of *c.* 1908.

Professor Sir ROBERT JENNINGS was knighted in 1981. He was elected President of the International Court of Justice in 1991, and awarded an honorary degree by the University in 1993.

RONALD ROLPH was Secretary of the Cambridge and District Trades Council. He worked for pensioners, civil liberties and world peace.

Dr SEDLEY TAYLOR (1834–1920) was Junior Bursar of Trinity 1866–9, Librarian 1870–1. Sedley Taylor Infant School, off Coleridge Road, is named after him, and he was a great promoter of music. The road is in a 'Trinity' area.

An Orphans' Cottage Home existed on Fitzwilliam Road, not far from [SHAFTESBURY] Road, which may commemorate the founder of charities, Anthony Ashley Cooper (1801–85), seventh Earl.

Sir William (Will) SPENS (1882–1962) was a scholar of King's, later Fellow and Master of Corpus Christi. He is remembered particularly for the 'Spens Report' on secondary education (1939) but was in 1939–45 regional commissioner for civil defence in East Anglia. In 1945 he was prominent in organising part of the new National Health Service. A formidable personality, 'Napoleonic' and 'Machiavellian' were adjectives applied to him by those with whom he worked, says the DNB. He was one of the most influential laymen in the Church of England, also 'surprisingly susceptible to female presence'.

SPRINGFIELD relates to a spring, as does the nearby Old Spring public house, and perhaps Overstream House by the river.

ST KILDA'S Avenue has at the corner with Campkin Road the pub, 'The Jenny Wren'. The island of St Kilda's is known for a distinctive type of wren, *troglodytes troglodytes hirtensis*.

STOCKWELL Street, HOPE Street and ARGYLE Street, turnings off Mill Road, have the same names as streets in the centre of Glasgow, where Stockwell Street and Hope Street are turnings off the main thoroughfare, Argyle Street. [COCK-BURN] Street, between Hope and Stockwell Street, is not the name of any street in Glasgow, but Henry Cockburn was elected Lord Rector of Glasgow University in 1831, and thus may have been meant here.

WILLIAM SMITH (see below, p. 141) Close, very near the above, but named much later, also relates to Glasgow.

STOTT is the name of the chief architect of the development of an estate, who had recently retired when the street was named.

SUN Street, parallel to Newmarket Road, borders the wood market of Stourbridge Fair once held here, and records the name of a pub now vanished.

SYMONDS Lane was named after Richard Symonds, or Jane his daughter, or both. He was a carrier and cattle-dealer, who lived in one of the cottages in 1864; she inherited the site from him. The present houses were built in 1938 by Miles Burkitt to help provide decent housing for village people.

THE CENACLE is named after the room in which the Last Supper was held. (Leonardo's painting of this event is Il Cenacolo; 'cena' means 'meal'. Answering objections, the developer said that the site was formerly the property of nearby St Mark's Church, and its shape, size and enclosed nature were appropriate.

According to a reliable account, when Councillors were not able to agree on a name, one of them produced his stapler, VELOS brand, said 'call it that', and they agreed.

The WELLBROOK Laundry, established on the Cambridge

Road, Girton, *c.* 1895 to serve Girton College, was still open in the 1980s.

WILDERSPIN is the name of a family who lived in the area of the street so-named until recent times.

In 1883 Sir WILLIAM SMITH founded the Boys' Brigade in Glasgow, in an attempt to improve the lot of local boys who were turning into criminals. Until recently the Brigade, attached to ST BARNABAS Church, used to parade through the streets with pipes and drums and wearing their 'pillbox' hats. The street was named after the founder in the centenary year at the request of the Brigade.

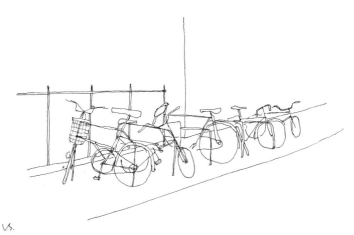

VS.

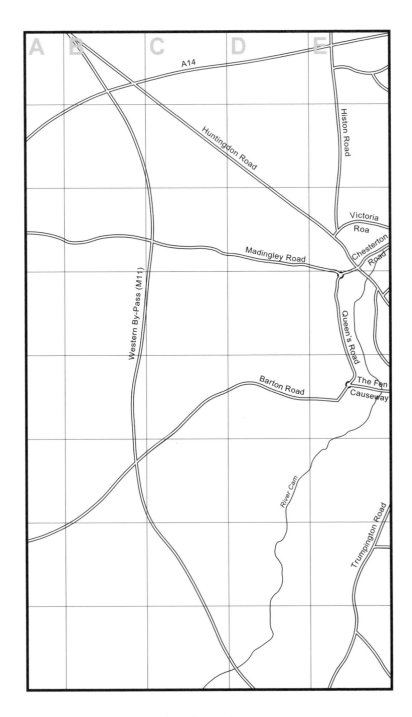

Plan of street locations
Streets in the Index are shown with a grid reference to the
Heffers/Ordnance Survey map of 1995. The same grid is used on

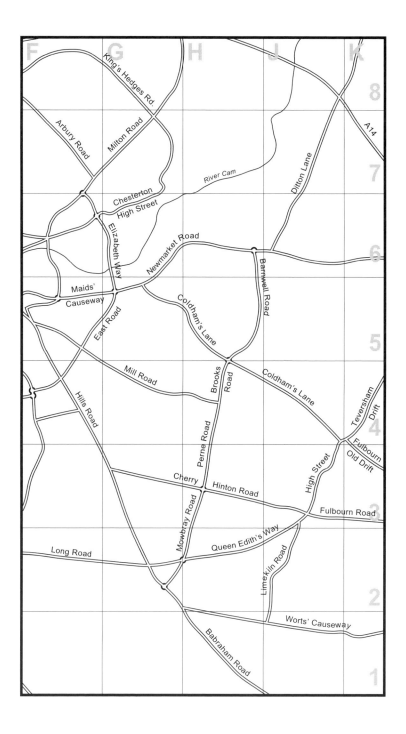

this map, so that anyone using a different map can locate the area in
which a street is situated and thence pinpoint it exactly.

Index of streets

The map references refer to the Ordnance Survey map of Cambridge published in 1995 in association with Heffers. No streets later than this are included, but a few which existed before and are not on that map are mentioned. Streets marked with a dagger (†) have names which can be found in gazetteers, but do not appear to have any notable Cambridge connection, except that some are the names of villages to which they lead. Others so marked are the names of houses, as well as of places, and most have probably some connection with the family or interests of a builder, developer, estate agent, given for a personal reason. Some personal names which do have Cambridge connections are of course also place-names.

Names that seem to need no explanation are marked with an asterisk (*). Streets in clusters of names of animals (see Antelope), wild flowers (see Clover) or apples (see Bramley) are marked with a double asterisk (**); those with names of stately homes, which are not in any clusters (see Arundel), are marked with a double dagger (‡).

145

Index of streets